Masterclass: Writing Romantic Fiction

Barbara Samuel

First published in Great Britain in 2014 by John Murray Learning. An Hachette UK company.

First published in US in 2014 by The McGraw-Hill Companies, Inc.

This edition published in 2014 by John Murray Learning

British Library Cataloguing in Publication Data: a catalogue record for this title is available from the British Library.

Library of Congress Catalog Card Number: on file.

Print ISBN 978 1 473 60042 3

eBook ISBN 978 1473 60044 7

10 9 8 7 6 5 4 3 2 1

The publisher has used its best endeavours to ensure that any website addresses referred to in this book are correct and active at the time of going to press. However, the publisher and the author have no responsibility for the websites and can make no guarantee that a site will remain live or that the content will remain relevant, decent or appropriate.

The publisher has made every effort to mark as such all words which it believes to be trademarks. The publisher should also like to make it clear that the presence of a word in the book, whether marked or unmarked, in no way affects its legal status as a trademark.

Every reasonable effort has been made by the publisher to trace the copyright holders of material in this book. Any errors or omissions should be notified in writing to the publisher, who will endeavour to rectify the situation for any reprints and future editions.

Typeset by Cenveo® Publisher Services.

Printed and bound in Great Britain by CPI Group (UK) Ltd., Croydon, CR0 4YY.

John Murray Learning policy is to use papers that are natural, renewable and recyclable products and made from wood grown in sustainable forests. The logging and manufacturing processes are expected to conform to the environmental regulations of the country of origin.

John Murray Learning
338 Euston Road
London NW1 3BH
www.hodder.co.uk

Also available in ebook

For Neal Barlow, aka Christopher Robin, who listens to endless variations on plot points over breakfast and comes up with ten more by supper, and doesn't ever mind when that supper is grilled cheese sandwiches for the seventh night in a row.

Acknowledgements

To travel well on this writing road, a writer needs teachers and compatriots and someone to pour a little more wine. Those who reached back to give me a hand forward are so numerous I am afraid to miss someone, but they include Leslie Wainger, Shauna Summers, Tara Gavin and Beth de Guzman; Kristin Hannah, Anne Stuart, Susan Wiggs, Roberta Gellis and Jennifer Crusie. I've travelled in great company, too, with Christie Ridgway, Liz Bevarly and Barbara Freethy, Susan Kay Law and Justine Davis, Jo Beverly and Connie Brockway. Here we are, still standing after all these years. The wine pourer will fill our glasses and I raise it to you, ladies. May we all write in good health and with great zest for decades more.

Contents

About the author

Barbara Samuel, who also writes as Barbara O'Neal, fell in love with food and restaurants at the age of 15, when she landed a job in a Greek café and served baklava for the first time. She sold her first novel in her twenties and has since won many awards, including two Colorado Book Awards and seven prestigious RITAs, including one for The Lost Recipe for Happiness *in 2010 and* How to Bake a Perfect Life *in 2012, which landed her in the Romance Writers of America Hall of Fame. Her novels have been published widely in around the world, and she travels internationally, presenting workshops, hiking hundreds of miles, and, of course, eating. She lives with her partner, a British endurance athlete, and their collection of cats and dogs, in Colorado Springs. Barbara also writes new adult romances as Lark O'Neal. Find her online at http://barbarasamuel.com or on Facebook at https://www.facebook.com/barbarasamueloneal*

Introduction

Welcome! You want to write a romantic novel – congratulations! It is one of the bestselling, most long-lived genres in fiction. In these pages you will learn about every aspect of writing a romance, from creating great characters and fresh plots to learning how (and when – or if!) to write sex scenes. You will do so through a carefully orchestrated set of workshops and writing exercises designed to take you step by step through each element of writing, and leave you with enough resources to carry you on through the rest of your writing and publishing journey.

This is meant to be a fast track to help you master the ideas and tools you will need to succeed in writing romantic novels – as if you were in a serious class with a group of other students, delving into the very bones of the genre, and uncovering and mastering the subtle tricks and layers of great romance. I am going to assume that you are a fan of the genre or you'd be reading some other book, and that you already know in your gut what you love and what you'd like to do, but feel the need for a few tools to get you going.

Various short and mid-length writing exercises in the book will help you focus on practical writing work related to each chapter's topic. These are as follows.

 Snapshots are short exercises or tasks related to the main idea in the adjacent text.

 Write exercises – self-explanatory – ask you to write focusing on a specific aspect of the craft of creating your story.

 Workshop exercises are longer exercises that ask you to do a bit more work – for example working out your characters' backgrounds.

 Edit is a reworking or review of a previous piece or exercise.

There are two other features within each chapter:

 Key ideas distil the most important points and ideas.

 Focus points at the end of each chapter distil that chapter's core messages.

Now, let's move forward to dive into the mesmerizing, popular, and very lucrative genre of romantic novels.

1

Understanding romantic novels

There is no other genre that is more polarizing, more beloved or more disdained than the romantic novel. I know this intimately after writing nearly 50 novels over 25 years, in virtually every subgenre of romance. The amount of revenue generated by romantic novels is well above that in other genres. What accounts for the vast popularity of these books, which have held their market share year after year, decade after decade, despite an ongoing (and undeserved) lack of respect from the rest of the literary world? Why do we so love to lose ourselves in a romantic story?

In this chapter you will learn some facts and figures about romantic novels as a genre; the reasons why romantic tales are beloved, even in a cynical society; and about the elements of a great romantic novel, to be discussed in more detail in later chapters.

How my story began

For me, it began like this. When I was a teenager, I babysat for the woman across the street. She worked late, serving cocktails at the local dog track, and I was sometimes there until three in the morning. She was a subscriber to Harlequin Presents, the classic romance category published in white covers, about men in Spain or Greece who said things like, 'You little fool,' just before they kissed the heroine passionately.

I adored these stories, read them one after the other after the other, sometimes two in an evening. Seeing my addiction, the woman gave me bags full of the books, and I took one bag on vacation with me. My grandmother drove her giant red Lincoln Continental across the western United States, and I sat beside her and read. I was 15 years old, and had already made my way through pretty much anything they'd let me check out of the library – all of Victoria Holt, Phyllis Whitney and Daphne du Maurier. I'd started making my way through my mother's historical novels, too, and earlier that year had read *Green Darkness* by Anya Seton, which I read an uncountable number of times (and still love).

But on that trip across the western United States in my grandmother's land yacht, I read Harlequin Presents by the ton. I read through a blizzard in Wyoming, in which we got stuck and had to be rescued by a trucker. I read through Idaho and through the pale-green and lush Columbia River Valley in Oregon. I read in tiny theme motels shaped like Alpine cottages and in the kitchenette where we finally landed in Seattle. I read about the Australian Outback and gloomy English country houses, about the Austrian countryside and, yes, castles in Spain.

 ## Key idea

Romantic novels are a massively popular arm of the market, worth more than $1,350 billion in sales in 2013 (source: Romance Writers of America).

A reader of the sort I was then (and still am) often evolves into a writer and, by the age of 15, I knew I wanted to write books. I knew that I wanted to be a novelist, though the word wasn't in my vocabulary at the time. I wanted to do a very specific sort of writing: stories about girls falling in love. I'd already written several by then, longhand in notebooks with pink or green or blue paper. (I would write only with a blue Bic pen, on college ruled notebook paper – a habit I kept until a journalism professor yanked the pen out of my hand and told me to go compose on a typewriter. Yes, a typewriter, and not even a particularly good one.)

On that trip with my grandmother, I was writing – endless, detailed journals about what I saw, absorbing details, paying attention. I can still remember what that blizzardy highway looked like, high in the mountains, cars piled up on the roadside like toys, and the giant of a man who clambered down from the cab of his semi-truck to drive us into safer territory.

This is what writers do, of course. I didn't realize it at the time, but it was the start of everything.

Jerry B. Jenkins

'Writers write.
Dreamers talk about it.'

When I returned home from my trip, I could hardly wait to go across the street to gather another paper sack full of romance. As I came into the living room with my haul, my father said, 'If you are so serious about being a writer, why don't you write a romance novel? I bet you could get it published.' (The subtext being: if I was 16 and a good writer, how hard could it be to write a romance?)

My heart woke up and started pounding at the idea of actually doing something like that. My mind, which generates story from anything, already began to toss out snippets and tidbits – probably a tall and brooding Spaniard and a stranded motorist on a blizzardy highway…

Unfortunately there were those who did not approve. My mother, who at the time would not even read a book that was popular enough to hit the bestseller lists, shuddered. 'She would never prostitute her talent that way!'

I blinked and looked at my mother, whose opinion mattered to me tremendously. The nascent dream shrivelled. I shut down any aspirations towards romance writing for years, until I'd gone through college, tried writing short stories and plays and all manner of other things. I was a struggling, poor, aspiring novelist with a degree in Mass Communications that I would have to put to good use if I couldn't figure out how to make money by writing.

Luckily, I am blessed with a sister who read all those Harlequins and Gothic romances along with me. She hadn't given them up for college, as I had. One day, she brought me two grocery bags full of new romances from her collection. This was the mid-1980s and the genre had grown hugely, proliferating into various new lines: Silhouette Special Edition and Desires, Harlequin Americans (my favourite at the time) and Silhouette Intimate Moments. Hundreds of romance novels were being published every month.

During my study years, the romance novels being published had matured and ripened. They were wide-ranging, no longer just castles in Spain and powerful men with brooding brows. These books showed a modern sensibility, with characters that had been divorced or had children. There might be a virginal heroine here and there but, more often, she was experienced. The characters were more realistic, more the kind of people I might know.

I peeled through them, and my excitement blossomed. Although I was still sending out boomerang short stories to literary magazines that would then pay me in copies of the magazine, and asking magazines for article assignments, I was half-hearted about those things. When I read these new romance novels, I knew in my gut that I could *do this*. I felt the beats in my blood and I could feel the flow of how it would go down on the page. I knew because of all that reading I'd done. I'd absorbed it into my bones.

My first attempt, however, was a clichéd mess. I took all those beats, took what I thought the genre wanted, sent it out, and promptly started another one. The words flew from my fingers. I couldn't wait to get back to my story every day. This second one was grittier, set in Pueblo, Colorado, around the steel mill that was collapsing at the time. The hero limped. The heroine was a widow who drank tea and composed music.

The first book made it through the channels at Harlequin, going up the chain, moving one direction and then another, though I had no idea of this at the time. I sent out the second book. The first was rejected, but at a very high level, by an editor who took the time to write me a letter about the book. I knew this was a Very Big Deal.

One year almost to the day after I had started the first romance, the second sold. It was two days before Thanksgiving in a blustery November almost 25 years ago as I write this, and it's a date I celebrate every year because that day – that book – changed my life. I never looked back or yearned for another kind of writing. I sat down in the romantic fiction chair and it fitted me just right. I've now written more than 45 novels – category, contemporary, historical, paranormal, women's fiction and New Adult / Young Adult – and all of the books have at their core a romance.

I hope you'll join me in exploring this world; maybe writing romantic novels will change your life, too.

Facts and figures

It cannot be denied that romantic novels are incredibly popular. Romance Writers of America collects statistics annually about the genre. As I write this, the most current statistics are from 2012, though you can read updates and notes at rwanational.org.

- Romance fiction generated $1,438 billion in sales in 2012.
- Romance was the top-performing category on the bestseller lists in 2012 (across the *NYT, USA Today,* and *PW* bestseller lists).
- Romance fiction sales are estimated at $1,350 billion for 2013.
- In 2008 74.8 million people read at least one romance novel (source: RWA Reader Survey).
- Romance fiction was the largest share of the US consumer market in 2012 at 16.7 per cent.

And there's this. While romance fiction generated $1.438 billion in estimated revenue for 2012, here are the figures for other genres for comparison:

- Religion/inspirational: $717.9 million
- Mystery: $728.2 million
- Science fiction/fantasy: $590.2 million
- Classic literary fiction: $470.5 million.

Those are some staggering differences. Some of the 2012 swell can be attributed to the explosive popularity of *50 Shades of Grey* but, even in the slower years, the differences are astonishing.

Why are romance novels so popular?

We are living in a society that values a cynical, sophisticated view of the world. We're so world-weary and knowing about everything that a romance sometimes seems impossibly quaint. We're overrun with divorce and 'hooking up' and texting break-ups and social mayhem of all sorts, after all.

We tell ourselves that we know what really happens to a lot of romance in the real world. Divorce and affairs, we say with sour faces. It's all Peter Pan men and disenchanted women, and nobody cares about the long term. And yet romance novels continue to be incredibly popular.

 Key idea

Even as we are spouting our cynical statistics and bemoaning the state of love in the world, people are desperate to connect. For all our social media, for all the shallow texting and chatter that goes on, we all long to be seen by others, to really know and be known. We yearn for union and happiness, so much so that people will pay for professional huggers to come over and lie down and hold them.

Human beings need love. We want love and sex and happiness and families. Finding love has a dizzying, heady, life-transforming power. Finding the right partner is also one of the biggest contributors to long-term happiness, which makes choosing that partner one of the most powerful decisions you will make in your life. Those are important ideas.

Romance novels are hopeful in a world that often seems to be full of crashing doom and despair.

Jennifer Crusie, who is one of the smartest women writing romance novels today (and believe me, there are many of them), has this to say about the power of romance novels:

Jennifer Crusie, *Romancing Reality*

'*Romance fiction places the woman at the centre of the story by refusing to pay lip service to the post-modernist view that life is hopeless and we're all victims. Instead, romance fiction almost universally reinforces the healthy human perception that the world is not a vicious tragic place, especially for women. This has been often cited as evidence that romance fiction does indeed dwell in a fantasy land, but showing women's victories is not unrealistic, nor is tragedy inherently superior or more realistic than comedy. This bias stems from an idea rife in literary fiction, best voiced by Joyce Carol Oates when she said, "Uplifting endings and resolutely cheery world views are appropriate to television commercials but insulting elsewhere. It is not only wicked to pretend otherwise, it is futile." Oates misses a serious point: it is as unrealistic to say that life is all tragedy as it is to say that life is all happy endings. The truth is, life is often both, and just as literary fiction usually opts for the tragic as the more dramatic and telling, so romance fiction, in choosing to show women readers the variety of possibilities in the real world of women's lives, opts for the happy ending as more empowering. Therefore the consistently satisfying endings of romance fiction, far from being unrealistic, actually bring balance back to the perception of reality by reminding the romance reader that, along with everything else, good things happen to good people, too, especially to strong, courageous women, especially when they work for it, at the centers of their own lives and stories.*'

Love stories have been with us from the dawn of time. David fell in love with a bathing beauty and upset the kingdom by pursuing her. His son, serious Solomon, wrote some of the most beautiful love poetry known to the Western world. Shakespeare gave us merry romantic comedies and heartbreaking romantic tragedies and sonnets by the dozen, all about love. And so did Austen and the Brontës, Heyer and Victoria Holt and Stephanie Meyer. Our movies are filled with love stories, too, and we flock to them, wanting to find again what we all know is true.

It feels wonderful – and terrible! – to fall in love. It makes fools of wise women and settles madmen. We know in our guts that it really matters, that there are few things, ever, that will match how we feel when we are falling in love. That's why we love romances.

 Connie Brockway

'No one ever fell in love gracefully.'

What makes a great romance novel?

It must be said that there are bad romance novels. There are bad novels of every type: rambling, self-important literary fiction, boring historical fiction, gratuitously violent action/adventure and thrillers. There is the same collection of excellence and trash in romance as in every other genre of fiction.

Instead, let's focus on the positive: what makes a great romance novel? What elements take a romantic novel from ordinary to magnificent? Personal preference enters into all reading, of course, and romances cover a huge spectrum of possibly great stories.

 ## Reflect on your own favourites

Take a moment and think of some of your favourite romances of all time. Some of mine are:

- *Green Darkness* by Anya Seton
- *The Shadow and the Star* by Laura Kinsale
- *On the Night of the Seventh Moon* by Victoria Holt
- *Night of the Phantom* by Anne Stuart
- *Not Quite a Husband* by Sherry Thomas
- *The Fault in Our Stars* by John Green.

In terms of movies (which I like to use in group settings and for discussion purposes as more people have seen individual movies than have read any one romantic novel), my top five are:

- *Love, Actually*
- *Titanic*
- *Green Card*
- *The Last of the Mohicans* (the version with Daniel Day Lewis): a movie so brilliant that it can be used to illustrate nearly every marker of great romantic stories
- *Romeo and Juliet* (the Zeffirelli version).

What makes these romances great? Why does *Pride and Prejudice* still work, all these years later? Why do we love *Romeo and Juliet*? What makes *The Last of the Mohicans* so absolutely brilliant? Why do I want to watch *Green Card* over and over and over again? Do all these stories – and your own favourites – have elements in common?

The common elements of romance fiction

It may seem mysterious, but each of these works has a very particular set of things in common. As with all good fiction, these elements are:

- great character development
- an understanding of theme and stakes
- a great setting and sense of place
- great writing
- a great voice
- a powerful sense of authenticity.

GREAT CHARACTER DEVELOPMENT

Great characters are unique, three-dimensional people who are connected to time, place, other characters and their own histories. How can a rake possibly be fresh? How can the middle-aged carpenter and his widowed mother seem like a new story? It's through the magic of powerful character development.

Alice in *The Last of the Mohicans* is a great study in character growth. She begins as a very proper English girl and, when things go badly, she's terrified and shy and a fainting maid in every way. Nothing in her life has prepared her to be brave, and she doesn't know how to handle the challenges she faces. At the end, when she makes her sacrifice in the great climactic scene that is so beautifully executed in the movie, she's being as brave as anyone ever has been. She's choosing her fate, rather than letting fate bob along with her in its clutches.

We will study character development in Chapter 4.

Your favourite characters

Write a list of your favourite romantic characters. What do you love about each one?

AN UNDERSTANDING OF THEME AND STAKES

A great romance novel also has great understanding of theme and stakes. It makes good use of detail to underline those themes and subtexts. In *Green Card,* we are not sure whether the hero really is a composer or just a big French oaf but, all through the movie, he's humming a little bar of music that's then translated into the theme of the story, which is about strangers becoming intimates.

The vicomte de Valmont, in *Dangerous Liaisons*

'And it's not that I want to have you. All I want is to deserve you.'

In *Dangerous Liaisons*, the hero is a rake who falls in love. The trouble is, his whole life has been based on keeping up appearances, and if he shows the world that he's genuinely fallen in love, he'll lose his standing as a great rake. If he doesn't show the world, he's doomed, and so is his lover. The stakes are enormous: life and death. In a way, all romances are based in that life-or-death equation.

Key idea

The reader needs to believe, really believe, that these two specific lovers are destined to be together, that nothing will really ever be right with them again if they don't get together, that they might even have been put on this earth just to be with each other.

We will discuss plot design in Chapter 5. We will discuss orchestrating emotion in Chapter 6.

A GREAT SETTING AND SENSE OF PLACE

This is an element that seems to be overlooked quite a lot, but I would argue that it's impossible to have a great romance novel without a great sense of place and setting. Setting is specific and particular, producing ideas and attitudes and character types of a specific sort. Creating a great setting offers a sense of verisimilitude to the reader, helping to connect her to the fictional world.

We will discuss setting and sense of place in Chapter 7.

Write about a place you love

Write a couple of paragraphs about a place you love and where you feel completely comfortable.

GREAT WRITING

You will work on your writing in the exercises throughout this book. This is a critical area, and I want to address the persistent idea that prose style doesn't matter much in a romance, as long as it is competent and clean. Clean and competent prose is not a terrible thing, but it will lead to merely competent romantic novels.

Your writing style matters tremendously. There's a mistaken idea that great prose is lyrical and calls attention to itself, but that's baroque and showing off. Great language is about making fresh choices, about listening to the rhythm of your work and to the book itself. Writer Christie Ridgway is a California native whose stories are always set in California, among the people and landscapes there. Her prose style is as lively and fresh smelling as a lemon grove.

We will discuss the tools of good writing in Chapters 9 and 10.

GREAT VOICE

Voice is perhaps my greatest passion in teaching students. It is not something you have to particularly work on, but set free. It begins with passion, with your interests and fascinations.

One of the books I've written that people cite over and over again as a favourite is *Jezebel's Blues*. It was my fifth book, a category romance for Silhouette Special Editions. It had a hideous cover, dark and muddy, and it didn't sell particularly well. But over and over again, readers express their love for this book in particular. It was my first finalist in the RITA Awards (a competition run by the Romance Writers of America (RWA)), and it made the lists of other awards that year.

When I wrote it, in 1991, I knew I was taking a chance by colouring outside the genre lines. It was a category book, after all. Musician heroes were frowned upon. But the story arrived practically whole, set in the East Texas milieu of my grandmother's stories, and to a soundtrack of the blues. There was a flood and two lonely people trapped in an attic for several days. It was a humid, musical story, and I wrote it with my full passion. I love the blues, I love cabin romances, and I loved the hero, Eric Putman, a wounded and lost bluesman, as much as I loved any character I'd created to that point. I wanted to bring more ethnic variety to category romance, too, and the town is a big stew of black and white characters.

I found my voice with that book. It showed, because readers connected and, even some 20 years later, it's one that still sells (though now with a much better cover).

That passion, that love of the material, is not something that can be faked. Readers can smell insincerity at a hundred paces, and respond to passion with an outpouring of passion of their own. If the writer is swept away, the reader will be, too.

This is not passion in the sense of sex, of course, but passion in the sense of that powerful love for the material, the subject and the setting. I know any number of people who want to write Scottish/Highland historical romances because they are so insanely popular, but it's easy to see who really loves the setting: writers with websites devoted to clan names, to tartans, to the psychology and politics of the time.

 ## What's *your* voice?

Writers love to fall in love with times, places, cultures and people. What are some of the things that interest you madly? What could you talk about for seven years without stopping?

We will discuss the writer's voice and how to recognize and capitalize on yours in Chapter 11.

A POWERFUL SENSE OF AUTHENTICITY

A great romance novel will feel true and unique. Of all the lovers in all of time, these two are unlike any others, and the reader believes in their story completely. That means there are no false notes of history, of language, of dialogue (see Chapter 10). Authenticity stems from all of the above, combined with the particularity of details that create your world (see Chapter 11).

> ## Key idea
>
>
> We can't afford to write a badly crafted romance.

I love romantic novels, and for that reason I want to see the best possible work in our genre. A badly crafted romance ruins the public perception of our books. It undermines the sheer power of our main theme (which is: love matters, love matters, love matters!). It makes of us less than we have the possibility to be.

It makes women's writing less than it can be, less than it should be. We have an obligation to make it as brilliant as possible.

Does that mean we have to write books according to what the (usually male) academic community believes they should be? No. These really are books about women's lives. Romances are women's fiction, and we're defining what women's fiction is even as we speak.

We're writing about what we care about.

Set up your study notebook

Every new venture requires a few supplies, and for this one you will need:
- a sturdy notebook with a ring binder
- loose-leaf paper to put in it
- a sheaf of dividers
- pens that flow and feel good in your hand.

When you get it home, set your notebook up however you like. Perhaps you like things to be very serious and tidy, or you want a beautiful photo on the front of the notebook to remind you of what it is you want to accomplish with your study of romantic novels. Don't worry about labelling the dividers yet. That will come later.

Timed writings

This notebook will be used to hold the exercises you will be prompted to write throughout this book. Many of them are timed writings.

I strongly believe in timed writings for a variety of purposes. Mainly, it is a practice that helps remove the editorial eye and chatter and allow creative thought to flow unimpeded. It's a simple process: set a timer for a specific amount of time and start writing. Then keep writing until the timer stops. That is the most important part of the process: to keep your hand moving across the page for the entire period, writing words. If you find you don't know what's next, write that: 'I don't know what comes next.' Often, what will arrive is, 'I don't know what comes next but I'm liking the idea of butterflies, blue, maybe flying over a field, maybe that's too stupid, but I'm thinking about it anyway.'

- Keep your hand moving. It will surprise you.
- Look for the prompts for timed writings throughout the book.

 Focus point

Why do you want to write a romantic novel? This is a good question to ask yourself at this point. Is it for money, for satisfaction, for fame or to fulfil a long-held desire? All answers are equally good. Be honest.

Where to next?

Next, we will take a look at the multitude of forms romantic novels take and the appeal of each one.

2

The different forms of the romantic novel

Romance novels are not one monolithic thing. There are dozens of forms, each with their own specific requirements and subtexts. How do you know what type of romance you are writing? Which form will your story idea take?

In this chapter you will learn about the many different forms of romantic novels, from the sweetest category of 200 pages to sweeping romantic epics of hundreds of pages that cross continents and even centuries. We will also discuss tropes of romances and romantic women's fiction, the more mainstream arms of the genre, as well as the various subgenres in romance and what each of them is all about.

The basic model

According to the Romance Writers of America, two basic elements comprise every romance novel: a central love story and an emotionally satisfying and optimistic ending.

 Key idea

Here's a definition of each of the two basic elements of the romance novel.

A central love story: The main plot centres around individuals falling in love and struggling to make the relationship work. A writer can include as many subplots as he/she wants as long as the love story is the main focus of the novel.

An emotionally satisfying and optimistic ending: In a romance, the lovers who take risks and struggle for each other and their relationship are rewarded with emotional justice and unconditional love.

These are working definitions but, for our purposes, romantic novels are defined more broadly. Many books are highly romantic without the romance being the central plot, although all commercial fiction readers are looking for the conservative ending: the world returned to order. That usually means an upbeat ending, and over-the-top happiness is great.

Romance novels may have any tone or style, be set in any place or time, and have varying levels of sensuality – ranging from sweet to extremely hot. These settings and distinctions of plot create specific subgenres within romance fiction.

The subgenres

Romance novels come in a multitude of sizes, styles and settings. The best way to understand the nuances is to read widely and deeply through the genre, of course, but here is a breakdown of many of the subgenres within romance.

SINGLE-TITLE ROMANCE

This is any contemporary novel not published by the category lines (see below) and usually quite a lot longer, from 75,000 to 150,000 words. Common forms include novels set in small towns, often a series of novels in the same small town, such as those written by Emily March, Susan Wiggs and Robyn Carr.

Other types are romantic comedies, such as those written by Christie Ridgway and Kristin Higgans, as well as any other contemporary romantic story in which the romance is the main plot (as opposed to women's fiction, below). There is nearly always a secondary plot that drives the story (for example, the hero or heroine has a troubled child or a failing business; or there is a need to save a building or local monument), as well as subplots involving other characters. A secondary plot can be a second romance, often involving characters less likely to be the stars, such as an older couple or a simpler conflict.

In a romantic series, there will often be long-term problems continuing over many books, too, such as struggles facing the town, or the problems of a single family.

Your basis for a series

Have you read a linked series of books? If you were to write one, would you prefer to use a town or a family as the organizing idea? Write a paragraph about that town or family.

ROMANTIC SUSPENSE

Any novel that includes a mystery, thriller or suspense plot in addition to the main romantic plot comes into this category. However, the focus will always be first on the romance and second on the suspense. This tradition began with the modern Gothic and writers such as Mary Stewart, Victoria Holt and Phyllis Whitney. It has continued to be popular in one form or another ever since. Some of the many current writers in the genre are Alison Brennan, Eileen Dreyer, Anne Stuart and Suzanne Brockmann.

Romantic suspense readers like a lot of action along with the romantic story, and it is important not to bog down the story with long descriptions or extended love scenes. The pace should be kept high.

Name your favourites

Do you enjoy romantic suspense, a little murder or mayhem along with your romance? Do you like a strong plot? Name some books you've enjoyed in this subgenre.

ROMANTIC WOMEN'S FICTION

This is an enormous category, perhaps the largest of all. It encompasses mainstream romantic stories of the type written by a vast number of writers, including Maeve Binchy (*Evening Class* is a particularly good example of her output), Kristin Hannah, Susan Wiggs, Eva Ibbotson and many others.

There are few rules to this sort of romantic story, other than there being something of a romance in the story somewhere. Often the story might star a somewhat older protagonist, or perhaps a group of protagonists, engaged in solving some life problem beyond romance. One recent example of this genre would be *The Best Exotic Marigold Hotel,* now also a movie.

A romance must still be part of the story but, in many cases, it is not the central story. Rather, the protagonist finds love and connection with a romantic partner as a reward for learning the lessons she needed to learn to progress to the next stage of her life. The themes can be dark or funny, with roots in the historical (Kate Morton, for example, writes a romantic tale often covering many decades, rooted in some thwarted or broken romance in the past) or the contemporary. Subjects cover a vast array of possibilities, too, such as the struggle with families or siblings, divorce and its aftermath, friendships between women, and the hunger to find a place in work and life.

This kind of book probably has the broadest appeal and continues to be published in large numbers. Book club readers love them (as most book club readers are women who enjoy a less harrowing story at times) – which offers an in-place marketing machine. The books are popular in libraries, too.

Nearly all traditional publishers publish women's fiction, including the highly successful Amazon Montlake programme. There have been some breakout bestsellers in women's fiction, but they are less visible than in other areas of romantic fiction, probably because of the book club angle, but that's just my theory.

NEW ADULT (NA) ROMANCE

This is a new and burgeoning genre about college-age women (18 to 24). As with women's fiction, there is often a focus on some lesson that is not romantic in nature, but there is always a romance, often quite spicy. It emerged directly from self-publishing, and many of the superstars of the genre (Colleen Hoover, Jamie McGuire, Jay Crownover) first published their books themselves and were later picked up by traditional publishers.

New Adult is almost entirely contemporary romance, often overflowing with angst and problems. There is an strong thread of working-class characters, tattoos, fighting and the hard living that come with making your way in the world without much to back you up. Another form that's edging into the market is the actual college romance, set on a campus and in dorms, with characters who are going to classes as well as partying. Look to writers like Viv Daniels and Megan Erikson for examples.

Finally, some New Adult is highly erotic, such as the novellas of H.M. Ward. Whatever form your novel takes, sex is part of what readers want, and probably a fair amount of it. If you consider that 18-to-24-year-olds have some freedom from their parents at last and that their biological imperative is to have sex as often as possible (in order to continue the species!), this makes a lot of sense.

Publishers who have done well with New Adult are Atria and William Morrow, but most publishers have come up with a way to publish this very popular form, and it is one of the most successful arenas of indie publishing.

Do a search

Do an Amazon or Google search for NA romance and read some of the descriptions and first pages. What leaps out at you? Is this something that appeals to you?

YOUNG ADULT (YA) ROMANCE

Romantic stories about teenagers can be historical, contemporary, paranormal or any combination of the above. Sex is often off-screen, but not always. This is one of the strongest areas of the field right now, full of inventive, richly textured stories including those by John Green and Gayle Forman. It's such a huge area that it's almost impossible to narrow the description down to a paragraph. If you're interested in this area, dig into the lists and you'll see what I mean.

Charlotte Bingham

'You can't write any form of fiction unless you enjoy reading it. You must be sincere in your approach. It's no good despising the rom. So many people think they could earn some money from writing something for which they have no affection. It won't work. The first thing you have to have is belief.'

HISTORICAL ROMANCE

This subgenre covers any novel set in a historical period. The most common eras are the Regency, Georgian and medieval periods, and such stories will nearly all be set in England, with perhaps some forays to as far away as France. The Victorian era is popular, too, and these stories may be set in England or America. American Westerns were dead for decades but seem suddenly to be having a resurgence. An era also in the ascendant is the early to mid-twentieth century, as more and more young writers are finding – through television shows like *Downton Abbey* – a passion for the times that their grandparents and great-grandparents had no interest in reading about.

Historical romantic novels have been a mainstay for generations. Writers such as Victoria Holt, Daphne du Maurier and Anya Seton were publishing novels in the 1960s and 1970s and, with the explosion of big sexy historical tales by writers like Kathleen Woodiwiss in the 1980s, the genre has been very strong for decades.

PARANORMAL AND FANTASY

This huge subgenre may include characters like vampires, shape-shifters, witches and elves, and magic, fantasy or science-fiction elements of many kinds. Very popular in recent years is urban fantasy, about magical beings and ideas in city settings. Also enormously popular, especially among young adult readers, is the dystopian fantasy, where the stories are set after an apocalypse of some sort. (All of this subgenre is often within the Young Adult category, above.)

EROTICA

These romantic novels are centred upon the sexual connection between the protagonists. The big star here is *50 Shades of Grey*, of course – one of the biggest bestsellers in history. For more in-depth information about this subgenre, see Judith Watts and Mirren Baxter's *Writing Erotic Fiction*, another title in this Teach Yourself series.

MIXING IT UP

Books can also combine subgenres, of course: YA can also be romantic suspense; NA can be paranormal and so on. When combining, be sure that you understand what the expectations of the reader in each arena are and satisfy elements of both.

'*Writing a category romance is like staging* Swan Lake *in a phone booth.*'

Category romance

Category romance deserves some special attention. Very few other forms of writing endure more disdain than the humble category romance, sometimes even within our ranks, but it is a remarkable form, and it gave me my start. I learned a tremendous amount about writing novels from writing category romance – from developing characters quickly to plotting the turning points to weaving in description and sexual tension.

It is also an arena that gave a huge number of women writers their start at a time when it was very difficult for us to break in, and especially writing novels about women's lives. I was in my mid-twenties, mother to two small boys and wife to a man who consumed 5,000 calories a day. I loved cooking for them all, growing flowers, making jam from the plums I bought at the farmer's market, but, when everyone else was asleep, I wrote by hand at the kitchen table, trying to find my voice. I knew I wanted to write fiction, but most of what I read was sad or dark and full of lessons not learned. I yearned to write something else, but I couldn't quite name it.

One gilded summer afternoon, the children were napping and I'd made plum jam and poured it into quilted jars. They were lined up on a stainless-steel counter, cooling, and every so often one would make the slight popping sound that meant it was sealed. I thought of my great-grandmother and how pleased she would be and how domestic life seemed important and real and somehow true to me. I wrote a short story I could never sell, called 'Texas, August and Other Mothers'. As I think of it now, it was filled with everything that would become the watermarks of my voice and work: the honour of a simple woman's life, the pleasure and power of food to connect us to one another, and the deep, sweet pleasure of being alive on a sunny August day.

Although the story never sold, it crystallized my desire to write about women's lives and concerns in a way that felt true to me. When I rediscovered category romances about three months later, I knew that I could tell stories about women winning, and finding happiness, and *those* were the stories that would be right for my voice.

There is an idea that romances of this sort raise unrealistic expectations in readers, but that's just foolishness. Women know what's real and what's not. A fantasy of a billionaire is just that – a fun, escapist fantasy. A category about an ordinary cop who falls in love with an ordinary baker, however – that is real life in a big way for a lot of people in the world.

WHO PUBLISHES CATEGORY ROMANCE?

Category or series romances are books published almost exclusively by Mills & Boon and Harlequin publishers. They are organized by line (Desire, Presents, Special Edition, Intimate Moments and others), which each have a specific word-count requirement, a clear expectation of material and a definite tone, ranging from sweet to sexy, small-town USA to glamorous cities and exotic locales like Greece, the Australian Outback and Africa. Hundreds of them are still published every year, affording new authors a chance to get their foot in the door. It's a great place to learn how to be professional and write to a deadline, to understand the editing process and learn to write a novel (just read the guidelines and you will learn a lot!) under the auspices of an editor and publisher. A writer must be professional and polished, of course, but because there are so many books on the calendar, there is also an opportunity.

You might recognize a few of these writers who started out in category romance:

- Suzanne Brockmann
- Sandra Brown
- Janet Evanovich
- Lori Foster
- Barbara Freethy
- Lisa Gardner

- Tess Gerritsen
- Tami Hoag
- Iris Johansen
- Jayne Ann Krentz
- Susan Mallery
- Jane Porter.

 Key idea

Category romance is written to very specific guidelines.

THE LINES AND THEIR REQUIREMENTS

To write for these lines, the writer must have a clear grasp of the expectations and the underlying myth or fantasy that each is expressing. Here is an overview of the lines and what they require:

- Harlequin American Romance

  55–60,000 words. Set in the United States, range of tones, strong family elements. Ranchers, cops and firefighters are popular types of hero.
- Harlequin Blaze

  60,000 words. Very sexy; the highest level of heat in all lines.
- Harlequin Desire

  50–55,000 words. Juicy, sensual, romantic. Set around the world, but should not feel exotic. (Just by perusing the titles, you will see that billionaires are popular in this line.)
- Harlequin Heartsong Presents

  45–50,000 words, featuring an evangelical Christian worldview. Two historical and one contemporary romance per month.
- Harlequin Heartwarming

  70–75,000 words. Clean, tender, loving, rather than sexy, but otherwise a complex story. Rated G for goodness.
- Harlequin Historical

  75,000 words. All time periods and sensuality levels welcome, from ancient Greece to 'the explicit bedroom romps of the Tudor times' to classic Mr Darcy.
- Harlequin Intrigue

  55–60,000 words. No graphic sex; hero and heroine solve a crime or mystery. Fast paced.
- Harlequin KISS

  50,000 words. Urban, contemporary, young and sparkling. Modern young women and their twenty-first-century alpha males.
- Harlequin Kimani Arabesque

  75–85,00 words. Single-title African-American romances presenting an upbeat, contemporary view of the characters.
- Harlequin Kimani Romance

  50,000 words. Sexy, sophisticated love stories about African-Americans set primarily in North America.
- Harlequin Kimani TRU

  60–70,000 words. Teen romance for African-American girls. True to life, with contemporary issues and conflicts.
- Harlequin Medical Romance

  50,000 words. Romances set in the medical world. This line seems to appeal more to the British than to North Americans, although the stories can be set anywhere.

- **Harlequin Nocturne**
  80–85,000 words. Action adventure romances set in a paranormal world with life or death stakes.
- **Harlequin Presents**
  50,000 words. The classic! A commanding hero, a feisty heroine, a glamorous setting around the world. Highly emotional stories.
- **Harlequin Romance**
  50,000 words. Another classic – settings are 'international and aspirational': you can 'travel the world with Harlequin Romance without leaving your armchair!' (Yes, yes; how many lands did I travel with Harlequin?)
- **Harlequin Romantic Suspense**
  70–75,000 words. This line was formerly called Intimate Moments, and it was one of the lines I wrote many books for. The emotional content is what packs a punch here, not the suspense, action or plot. That said, the stories should contain danger and excitement.
- **Harlequin Special Edition**
  55–60,000 words. Another line I wrote for. If the small-town series contemporaries have a mother, this is where they began. Susan Mallery, one of the superstars of small-town romance, began writing for this line. Warm, with lots of classic themes.
- **Harlequin Superromance**
  85,000 words. Big, believable romance with broad scope. Settings are primarily North American but can be elsewhere, with cities as well as small towns welcome locations.
- **Love Inspired: LI Historical and LI Suspense**
  Various lengths. with Christian characters and values facing historical problems or romance, or suspense-driven plots.

Whew! You see what I mean?

 ## Read the Harlequin guidelines

Guidelines are available for all lines at harlequin.com and I suggest you check the website for the most current information. Read the guidelines, at least a few of them. Are you intrigued or turned off? Do you find yourself drawn to wanting to write for one of the lines?

Tropes

Every genre has its favoured themes and motifs, or tropes – even literary fiction, which claims not to have them. Understanding what some of the tropes are and why they are appealing can be a helpful underpinning in your work. We all gravitate to some more than others, both as readers and writers. As I've said elsewhere, I never got over *Romeo and Juliet*, so I have a deep and abiding affection for forbidden love, whether it's based in class or race or culture or alien/human, but I also love a great road or cabin romance, lost lovers reunited and, much as it pains me to admit it, the bad boy (or rake) tamed. Oh, and amnesia. Also, a great marriage-of-convenience story can make me swoon.

Think about the tropes you love in the genre. If I consider my tastes, forbidden love works for me because I like the idea of two lovers united against the world. It's highly romantic. I love amnesia for the idea of second chances, and reinvention. Road and cabin romances force close proximity and a step away from normal life, and marriage of convenience speaks to my need to believe in fate, but also in the practicality of being able to love.

Bad boys tamed… sigh. Why do I love them so? In real life, they're prison bait and probably drink too much and are never going to stick around. In real life, they are everything your father worries they are. But in a romance, bad boys are untamed and exciting and you just know that they'd know their way around a woman's body, and even if you were not the woman who could bring him to his knees, the fantasy is appealing. He will love only… *me*.

We don't all love the same tropes, thank goodness. What are yours?

Your favourite tropes

Look at the list below. What are your favourites and what is so appealing about them? This is by no means a complete list. Can you add to it?

Forbidden love	Marriage of convenience
Barbarian or stranger and the innocent	Ugly duckling
	Cinderella
Guardian/ward	Sheik romances
Friends to lovers	Billionaires
Lost lovers reunited	Boss/secretary

Revenge	Mistaken Identity
The love triangle	Cabin romances
Enemies to lovers	Secret baby
Bad boy tamed	Amnesia

Many of the above tropes are present in romantic historical fiction and romantic women's fiction, and they can carry even more power if you are able to somehow ground them in a world that is not a fantasy but true to life. In women's fiction, lost loves, revenge and love triangles can take on strong undertones, but a very big one is second chances.

Turn tropes on their heads

Examine the list of favourite tropes above. How can you take one or two of them and turn them on their heads? Can a cabin romance happen in a busy hotel? Can the bad boy be a bad girl? Where would that story be best published?

Workshop

Take an hour or two and head over to your local bookstore and spend some time browsing the romance shelves.

- Can you find examples of each of the subgenres listed here?
- What sort of covers does each of them have?
- What sorts of plotline are usual?

Buy a few in a subgenre you enjoy, and take them home to read. (For more on studying and breaking down the elements of a romance novel, see Chapter 3.)

Alternatively, you can study books online, at a site such as Amazon or iBooks. This is a good way to examine cover treatments and plotlines, so that you can both understand the nuances of each style of romance, and then create fresh variations of your own. Read the first pages or the first chapter to get a feeling for the spirit and tone of each book.

In your study notebook, record your impressions. Is one area more appealing than others? Did anything surprise you?

Where to next?

In the next chapter, we will look more closely at how to deconstruct and understand all the elements of various romantic novels.

3

Studying the genre

The single most important thing you can do to understand any form of writing is to read. Read widely and read deeply, and you will begin to understand how fiction works. All fiction follows certain paths, covers some of the same ground, and nearly everything we read follows a similar pattern, ingrained over millennia of storytelling: a character who is called to trouble, and either overcomes it or fails.

In this chapter you will learn how to read like a writer: you will find out how to deconstruct a romantic novel in order to understand the elements that make it work, and use a worksheet to understand the 'beats' of a novel.

W.P. Kinsella

'Read! Read! Read! And then read some more. When you find something that thrills you, take it apart paragraph by paragraph, line by line, word by word, to see what made it so wonderful. Then use those tricks the next time you write.'

What reading teaches us

Most of us come to our genre through reading, of course. Just as I spent those long nights babysitting and reading endless Harlequins, you might have come home from work or school to absorb every Scottish Highlander romance or saga or women's fiction or chick lit novel you could get your hands on. Reading teaches us what the promises are: in chick lit, the plucky, slightly lost heroine will lose a guy, find a guy, and figure out more about herself and her work and her goals by the end of a book. In domestic novels, a woman might discover herself again after many years of serving others.

 ## Key idea

In romantic tales, the hero always wins, even if she arrives back home battered and weary.

To understand the subtleties of your particular genre, you must read it deeply. Don't confuse the beats (the individual turning or action points) with dramatic clichés, either – a common mistake, and one I made myself with my first attempt at category romance. Most of us begin by imitating what already exists, what we've read, and that's perfectly right. By reading a lot, you will learn where the clichés are ('If I read one more [fill in the blank], I'll scream!') and how to build on the expected beats to create something fresh and new.

 ## Key idea

By reading copiously in a chosen area, the writer absorbs the beats by osmosis. You will hone your instincts for turning points, how to pause and how to move forward, when to introduce key characters and conflicts, and how much or how little description, dialogue and setting is usual.

Write a clichéd scene

Write a scene that utilizes a dramatic cliché in an exaggerated way. Pull out all the stops with every means at your disposal – description, prose and characterization.

Ray Bradbury

'*When I graduated from high school I couldn't go to college, so I went to the library three days a week for ten years.*'

Deconstruction

Key idea

To best understand anything, one should study. Intently.

When I first began to write romances, I had just finished four years at university, where I'd spent virtually every day taking things apart, examining the bits and pieces, then trying to fit them back together again. I'd done it with botany and sociology, fiction and newspaper stories, physics and psychology. It therefore made sense to deconstruct romance novels in the same way, to understand how they fit together. I read and studied dozens and dozens of romantic tales. It was an enormous help to me in finally working out the ideas and structure of romance.

I am not alone in this. Jennifer Crusie famously tells the story of a graduate project. She went to bed one weekend with 100 romance novels, intending to study them for female narrative structure, and got out of bed the next week a romance writer – and a very, very good one. If you enjoy snarky humour, tough love, and an absolutely unsentimental view of love and sex – even as it carries her characters away – you will love Cruisie. (Start with *Welcome to Temptation*, a tale of a handful of women making a porn film, or the RITA-award winning *Bet Me*, my personal favourite.)

Deconstruction is a time-honoured method of understanding anything and it will play an important part in your study of romantic novels. I will help you deconstruct a few romance novels as we go. You may already have favourite books you wish to study, or you may have found some titles on your bookstore outing (see Chapter 2). I have included an appendix with several lists of the best romances. One is a list of the Romance Writers of America's Hall of Fame winners, writers who have all won three RITAs in a single category. Another is a list of 'the 100 best romances' as assembled by buzzle.com, which I chose simply because it is a widely varied compilation, if a little dated. I've also included a list of my own favourites. I'm a voracious and passionate reader, and have read in nearly every arena of romantic fiction for several decades. There are many other 'best of' lists online, at 'Dear Author' and 'All About Romance' and others. It doesn't matter which lists you examine.

 ## Choose three books to study

Choose three books to examine as we move through these pages. These should be books you have deeply enjoyed reading, books you would like to emulate, or books you simply want to read. (It may also be helpful to study books you find loathsome, in order to understand why they failed.)

I've chosen two books to use as examples as we move through the exercises, one historical and one women's fiction. Both are easily available if you care to read them and follow along. The first is *The Shadow and The Star*, by Laura Kinsale, a highly regarded historical romance set in Victorian England and Hawaii. The second is my own *The Lost Recipe for Happiness*, by Barbara O'Neal, which won the RITA award and was reprinted nine times. It is romantic women's fiction.

Below is a blank worksheet I've designed to help you understand the elements of romance novels. Don't be overwhelmed. There may be things on the worksheet that you don't understand, and that's fine. As my t'ai chi instructor always reminds us, it is impossible to be an expert at something when you are beginning.

Workshop

For one of the novels you've chosen, complete the following worksheet. Do your best, and know that you will come back to this worksheet later with a much better understanding of what it means. If something feels daunting or overwhelming, just skip that step for now. Fill in what you can and leave the rest for another time.

WORKSHEET FOR DECONSTRUCTING ROMANCE NOVELS

Book title	
Author	
Publisher	
Date of publication (this is important as tastes change over time)	
Subgenre	
What is the location of the book?	
What is the year?	
What is the basic set-up? Who are the main characters?	
The hero	
The heroine	

The antagonist/villain	
What does the hero need to accomplish to be happy/satisfied?	
What stands in his way?	
What does the heroine need to accomplish to be happy/satisfied?	
What stands in her way?	
What is the hero/heroine's internal journey about? (What does she need to feel whole, apart from her love life?)	
If there is no identifiable antagonist, can you identify the force opposing the lovers' happy ending?	
Who are the secondary characters?	
What role does each of them play? (Best friend, ex-lover, antagonist?)	
How do hero and heroine meet?	
On what page?	

How sensual is this book? (Sweet, sensual, sexy, erotic, erotic++)	
What is the main conflict between the characters? When do we learn what that is?	
What other conflicts do they face?	
Orchestrating the emotion	
When is the first touch and what is it?	
When is the first kiss?	
When is the first love scene (either interrupted or completed)?	
How many love scenes are there? How long is each one?	
What is the dark moment?	
What is their happy ending?*	
Point of view	
Who tells the story? (hero, heroine, both, others)	

Is it in first person/third person?	
Is it in the past tense?	

Writing style

How would you rate the actual writing in this book?	
Is the prose lush, spare? Short sentences, long sentences?	
Is it easy to read or more elaborate?	

Analysis

What works in the story?	
What is weak or undermines the tale?	
What is your overall rating? Why?	
Finally: what do you like about this book? What works for you as a reader? If it is a terrible book, write about what is terrible.	

*If there is no happy ending, how does the tragedy return life to a better balance? (This is an important aspect of a tragedy – readers hate it when a character dies or the romance ends badly, so there must be a very, very good reason; tragedy must serve the task of righting wrongs more satisfyingly than happiness. This, I warn you, is very rare.)

Now let's take a look at how the worksheet looks when it is completed. I've filled it in for my own *Lost Recipe for Happiness* as an example of how the process works.

WORKSHEET EXAMPLE

Book title	*The Lost Recipe for Happiness*
Author	Barbara O'Neal
Publisher	Bantam Books
Date of publication (this is important as tastes change over time)	2009
Subgenre	Women's fiction with romantic elements
What is the location of the book?	Aspen, Colorado and northern New Mexico
What is the year?	Current day
What is the basic set-up? Who are the main characters?	A female chef is invited to open a restaurant with a movie director who has been her boss
The hero	Julian Liswood, a successful director of horror films and restaurateur
The heroine	Elena Alvarez, a woman with a tragic history, and a chef eager to make a name for herself
The antagonist/villain	The past and Santino, the malcontented chef Elena displaced
What does the hero need to accomplish to be happy/satisfied?	He wants to open a new successful restaurant in Aspen. He's also trying to make a good life for his 15-year-old daughter.
What stands in his way?	His daughter is dissatisfied and has been in trouble. He is also haunted by his mother's murder, which informs and shapes his horror films.
What does the heroine need to accomplish to be happy/satisfied?	To open a successful restaurant with her own vision, and put the past and her ghosts to rest.
What stands in her way?	Her need to stay connected to the people she lost in a terrible car accident, including her sister and the boy she loved.
What is the hero/heroine's internal journey about? (What does she need to feel whole, apart from her love life?)	Elena must let go of her grief in order to live her life. She wants very much to have a new love in her life, and to be a success as a chef with her own menu.
If there is no identifiable antagonist, can you identify the force opposing the lovers' happy ending?	

Who are the secondary characters?	The main secondaries are Santino, a gay chef with a dark past; Julian's 15-year-old daughter; and the ghost of Elena's sister.
What role does each of them play? (Best friend, ex-lover, antagonist?)	Santino is Elena's antagonist; he's been pushed aside and wanted to be head chef. Elena's sister is her best friend, her most constant companion. Julian's daughter is both antagonist and friend, a complication but also a draw for Elena, who sympathizes with her.
How do hero and heroine meet?	He's her boss and offers her a job.
On what page?	Page 3
How sensual is this book? (Sweet, sensual, sexy, erotic, erotic++)	Sexy. There are several detailed sex scenes. It is a very sensual book, detailing how Elena comes back to life through food and sensual connection to Julian.
What is the main conflict between the characters? When do we learn what that is?	The main conflict is that Elena must let go of the past, and at first she doesn't even realize that she has not done so.
What other conflicts do they face?	He is her boss and will fire her if the restaurant fails. He has written her story into a script and is afraid she will be angry. She has reservations about getting involved with a man with so much wealth and power. How could he possibly love her for the long term?
Orchestrating the emotion	
When is the first touch and what is it?	A kiss
When is the first kiss?	40 per cent of the way through
When is the first love scene (either interrupted or completed)?	63 per cent of the way through
How many love scenes are there? How long is each one?	Several, at least four pages
What is the dark moment?	When Elena comes to a crisis and has to return home to face her demons, and Julian must reveal the secret he has been keeping
What is their happy ending?	When Elena bids farewell to her ghosts and returns to Aspen, much healed

Point of view	
Who tells the story? (hero, heroine, both, others)	Mostly the heroine; sometimes the hero
Is it in first person, third person?	Third person
Is it in the past tense?	Past tense
Writing style	
How would you rate the actual writing in this book?	Strong, fairly descriptive
Is the prose lush, spare? Short sentences, long sentences?	More long than short, but a mix. It is magic realism, so there is a lot of colour and poetry.
Is it easy to read or more elaborate?	Easy reading
Analysis	*I'll leave the analysis to others.*

Rewrite your clichéd piece

Return to the piece you wrote utilizing and exaggerating a cliché of romantic fiction. Rewrite it to express true emotion and authenticity. Now go back through it: what words did you change? What did you have to shift to make it read like something real?

Write about a novel

Write about one of the novels you've chosen. Why did you choose it? What appeals to you most about it? Was it character, setting or a particular kind of conflict? If you had written the book yourself, is there anything you would have changed?

Focus point

Deconstructing a novel helps a reader to become a writer by letting them identify the different parts so that they can truly understand them, much in the way that a budding mechanic takes apart a machine to see where the wires go and how the gears move. In the next few chapters, we will examine each of those gears, wires and other elements so that you can then construct your book with a clear understanding of how everything fits together.

In the next chapter, we will explore one of the most basic elements of any good novel: how to create powerful, believable characters.

4

Creating believable, powerful characters

Every romantic plot is essentially the same arc: two people meet, fall in love, struggle against either the external or the internal forces keeping them apart, and then finally get back together and live happily ever after. The reason we continue to read such novels – even those in the same subgenre – is because each pair of lovers is unique. Each human, paired with any other, creates a different couple, a different story and a different arc. This is why character is the soul of romantic novels.

In this chapter we will examine the elements that create great characters, how to craft characters the reader will remember and how to use tools such as autobiographies and character interviews to workshop a character of your own creation.

William Faulkner

'It begins with a character, usually, and once he stands up on his feet and begins to move, all I can do is trot along behind him with a paper and pencil trying to keep up long enough to put down what he says and does.'

Heroes and heroines

Let's take a moment to consider some of the great pairs of lovers in romances we love: Scarlett O'Hara and Rhett Butler in *Gone with the Wind*; Romeo and Juliet; and Jack and Rose in *Titanic*.

These are all three tragic examples, but in each case most of us are familiar enough with the main characters to at least understand the context. Scarlett and Rhett are an excellent example of two fatal flaws colliding. She's spoiled and wilful and in love with someone else. He is a ladies' man who is used to charming the stockings from the females in his world, but Scarlett is his match. The trouble is that they both fall in love with each other but realize it too late. Pride breaks each of them in a different way.

The point is, however, that, if I say 'Scarlett O'Hara', you know exactly what sort of woman I mean, very specifically. She is flawed, but she's also powerful. She is tested to within a millimetre of breaking but, because we know and understand her character, we know she will eventually survive. We also know that she will lose everything because she can't see herself clearly.

Study the lovers in a movie

Watch *Titanic*, or any other romantic movie of your choice, and pick out the differences and similarities between the main characters. Make as many notes as you can.

Romeo and Juliet are very young, and more placeholders for Young Lovers Who Are Manipulated by Their Families than unique, developed beings, but we know the tale by the fact that they are from opposing families. He is an inconstant lad, falling in love at the drop of a hat, but finds Juliet the most compelling of all girls. She is an innocent swept away by passion and powerful words and kisses stolen from a balcony. The point of the tale is that grudges cause terrible loss, which in this case causes 'a glooming peace' with the death of the young lovers.

Forbidden love is one of my favourite themes in romance, and it is generally given its power through the specifics of the forbidden tale. I have worked with it quite a lot, most often using cultural and/or racial divides (*The Sleeping Night, A Bed of Spices*), but I've also used class divisions, as in *Heart of a Knight*. It becomes very important to the reader to understand why these two particular people are drawn to each other and will risk everything to make a life together. Why *this* person when all it will do is make everyone around them miserable?

Write a character sketch

Who are some of your favourite heroes in romantic novels? Write a character sketch about one of them. Include all the reasons he is memorable, and what makes him tick. What drives him? What does he fear?

In *Titanic*, Jack and Rose are also forbidden lovers, for economic reasons. Jack is a charming artist who wins his passage in a card game. Rose is one of the elite on the ship, engaged to a very powerful and wealthy man.

Rose is in despair as the movie opens. She feels she's being sold – and, in a very real sense, she is. When Jack talks her down from her suicide attempt, the two feel an immediate bond beneath the cold starry skies of the Atlantic. She is beautiful and naive. He is charming and experienced. Each offers something to the other that is a lure. Over the next few days, this connection grows. He discovers that she yearns for adventure and a life lived on her own terms. She learns that he has done exactly that. She discovers that he's smart and resourceful when he comes to dinner in her world. He learns that she can let her hair down and dance exuberantly when she comes below decks. They fall in love with the differences between them, but more with the similarities. Each feels freed by the other. Jack's art is given importance when Rose offers herself sensually to him, and her sensuality is given full rein by his respect for her.

The analysis can go much deeper.

Deconstruct a character

Choose a character from one of the novels you have been deconstructing and answer the following questions:

1 What are the three primary traits of this character? Rose, for example, is rich, beautiful and tied into a straitjacket.
2 What are the main flaws of this character? (Sometimes this is a little harder to discover.) Rose's main flaw is her inability to stand up to her family and circumstances.

Building characters from scratch

Seeing the possibilities in character and then being able to transfer that knowledge to the page are two different things. What are the building blocks you need to create fresh, original, unique characters of your own?

Key idea

Characters are specific.

In workshops all over North America, I play a game by asking writers to raise their hand and give me their Starbucks order. I used to have to drive quite a lot between two towns many miles apart. My order was a triple venti skim latte with five raw sugars. In those days, I was running on empty most days, juggling family and work and romantic life in a scary balancing act that threatened to fall into disarray at any moment. Guzzling caffeine and sugar gave me the boost I needed to power through. These days, my order is a much more modest grande soy 1/2 vanilla latte: still some coffee, still some sugar, but not so much.

That's a good character detail, but there is more. In the first instance, if I had to go through the drive-up, I'd order the sugars, but I'd always have to make a joke about it to alleviate my embarrassment and acknowledge that it was *a lot* of sugar, even in that much coffee. If I went inside, I'd pile the packets together so that no one watching would see how many it was, and tear off the tops all at once.

Starbucks is so very, very American. It buys into that whole sense of entitlement to having things exactly the way you want them: my triple venti latte with skimmed milk, vanilla syrup and five raw sugars (not white sugar, not Equal or Splenda or Sweet'n Low, but raw cane sugar, which says I care about the environment or natural foods or I just like being cool), not to mention the whole American ideal of capitalizing on capitalism by figuring out a way to get people to pay ten times what a cup of coffee used to cost just to make them feel groovy doing it.

Write about three characters

Write a paragraph about the people who order three different drinks at a coffee shop. Who orders a fancy milkshake? Who has tea with milk, no sugar? Does one eschew the chain coffee shop for the non-corporate indie bookstore? Does she find it ridiculous or embarrassing to order complicated things and defiantly orders straight black coffee, nothing else?

Remember that the coffee is just one layer. Take it deeper and then deeper again. Remember that people are complex beings.

The first time I talked about the Starbucks order, I was going to Vancouver, and I suddenly worried that there might not be a Starbucks there. I went on the Web to see whether there was and if and where in that city it might be. I stopped counting at 130 something, including two across the street from each other.

The reason I could do that was because some guy on the Internet has gone around the world taking photos of every Starbucks he can visit. On his site I spotted my own local Starbucks, and both of the ones I visit in Colorado Springs, and some in London! How's that for characterization? Who does that? Why does he do it? What's going on with him?

Gore Vidal

'Each writer is born with a repertory company in his head. Shakespeare has perhaps 20 players… I have 10 or so, and that's a lot. As you get older, you become more skilful at casting them.'

Making characters memorable

The Last of the Mohicans has a great cast of characters: the two sisters, Alice and Cora; the noble British soldier; the Last Mohican and his son; their antagonist Magua; and, last but not least, Hawkeye. Every character has a goal, and some goals are thwarted, some are achieved, but they weave together in a gorgeous dance.

As we saw in Chapter 1, Alice, the younger sister, is an example of a character who is memorable because she evolves and grows. She changes from being a very proper, timid English girl who has lived a sheltered life into someone who faces an impossible situation with extreme fortitude. At the end, when she chooses to go over the edge of the cliff rather than go with a man she despises, she's being as brave as anyone ever has been.

While good romantic fiction makes great use of character detail to underline its themes and subtexts, the reader also needs to feel that the specific lovers in the story are unique individuals with rich, vivid lives. The reader needs to believe in these two characters because of who they are, and that because of who they are they are destined to be together and that nothing will ever be right with them again if they don't get together.

Write about yourself as a character

You are a character yourself, as is everyone around you. Write a character sketch about yourself. What makes you memorable, authentic, complex and unique?

A MEMORABLE CHARACTER IS SPECIFIC

She's not a general, generic, please-everyone kind of person. She's born into the book world with very specific, very detailed wishes, wants, dreams, goals, hopes, hungers, tastes, flaws and vices.

A MEMORABLE CHARACTER IS AUTHENTIC

A great character is a product of her time and place. A person born in a small farm town in the American Midwest is not the same person as a person born and raised in a small farm town in England or Oregon. When creating characters we must take into account the fact that weather, cultural norms and landscape strongly influence the way people view the world.

A MEMORABLE CHARACTER HAS DEPTH

She has history and a past and a life that started before the book and goes on after the book. She has connections to other people. She has memories and flaws and treasures.

Get to know your character

What are the engaging, everyman or everywoman qualities in your character? What are their unique qualities? Can you see two sides to this character?

A MEMORABLE CHARACTER IS SYMPATHETIC

We must be able to walk around in the skin of a fictional character, for good or ill.

I am fascinated by why Tony Soprano, a fat, violent, ruthless killer, is so sympathetic. He breathes too loudly. He smokes cigars. He cheats on his wife. There was one episode, early on, when he was revealed as an absolutely unforgiving mob boss, killing a child who really only kind of deserves it, and I found myself, watching, horrified – and making excuses for him.

Why? Because I can relate to Tony Soprano. We all can. He's a guy with a lot of responsibilities and a high-pressure job. He suffers panic attacks. He loves his children. He really has a big kind heart and, in a lot of ways, he's a really just a big, loveable bear of a guy. When he's not, you know, killing people.

As I writer, I started to pay attention to what details were making me like him, and there were many. He really listens when people talk to him. He's a toucher, he puts his hands on people in gentle ways. By the standards of his world, he has absolute integrity. He rules his kingdom and his world with fairness and honour. He tries to prevent wars and unnecessary killing. He rewards loyalty. And he has an absolutely horrible mother whom he still wants to please.

We should all be so talented as to create a character as compelling as Tony Soprano. Few of us ever will, but we should eternally be striving towards it.

Key idea

Don't be afraid of dichotomy and really digging into the reality of your characters. Pull out the stops. You can always pull back later.

Make your character more compelling

Return to the character sketch you wrote about yourself. How can you exaggerate some elements of your personality to make the character more interesting on the page? What can you tone down? What can you add to make this other self more sympathetic to your reader? Is there a habit that others might identify with? Can you expand on a flaw or make it worse?

Workshop

Label one of the dividers in your notebook 'Character building', and let's find out as much as possible about each of your characters. The more clearly you understand the book person you are creating, the more easily you can work with him on the page, move as he moves, choose breakfast as he does, understand what he would say to someone and how he would react in any given situation. By the end of a book, you should be able to walk into a department store and choose clothes for your main characters.

Completing the character sheet below will help you get to know your character thoroughly. Feel free to add further questions. You may find it useful to create copies of the list of questions before you start, so that you can use it again and again.

I was trained as a reporter, so I tend to phrase these questions in the form of an interview, and let the character answer in the first person, as in 'I was born in a tiny village by the edge of the sea.'

CHARACTER INTERVIEW

Background	
What's your name?	
Where were you born?	
Who are your parents?	
Do you have siblings?	
What is your birth order (first, middle child, baby)?	
Where did you grow up?	
What is your family's ethnic background?	

What did you want to do with your life when you were 15?	
What are your religious leanings?	
If you could go to any country in the world for one month, where would it be, and why?	
Present day	
How old are you?	
What do you look like?	
What do you do for work?	
How do you feel about that work?	

CHARACTER INTERVIEW

Where do you live?	
Have you ever been married?	
Who is your best friend?	
Who is your worst enemy?	
What's the happiest memory you can think of?	
What's the darkest moment of your life thus far?	
What are your political affiliations?	
What are your spiritual or religious leanings?	

Creating character backgrounds

Setting and sense of place will influence your characters and the way you create the landscape of your novel. Many of my characters are from the American West because I know it so well, but there's no reason not to go far as afield as you want to.

The three elements of creating character backgrounds are physical, cultural and spiritual:

- **Physical** refers to the landscape, the weather, the plants and animals, and the geography.
- **Cultural** refers to the groups who live in an area, their manners and morals, their language sets and accents, and the specific character types we'll discover in that world.
- **Spiritual** refers to the overall soul of place.

(We will delve into this in more depth in Chapter 7.)

 Laura Ingalls Wilder

'Home is the nicest word there is.'

Part of what we're doing in romantic tales is extending a fantasy – our hero might be a Navy SEAL or an exotic foreigner, a rich restaurateur or a darkly handsome lord. In my novel *Lady Luck's Map of Vegas* the heroine's love interest was Irish – specifically he was Gabriel Byrne, on whom I had a painful crush. I also have a thing for accents, and I can 'hear' an Irish accent more easily than some others, so I thought – well, why not? Let's make him Irish from Ireland.

This meant that I had to work out a family history against a background I wasn't particularly familiar with. I had been to a small city in Scotland with a native, and saw the acres of council houses there, and listened to the family's stories of growing up in that world, and I knew that, although there would be differences, I could at least generalize some of it. I read about the city of Galway and I'd travelled in western Ireland, so I knew what it looked like. I just sketched his family history in broad strokes, and it was OK.

Don't be afraid to enjoy yourself on this level, and let your imagination take flight. I once wrote a character for a romantic suspense line who was the daughter of an American racing driver. I had to imagine what it would be like to have a father who was engaged in such a dangerous profession. It was a lot of fun to write.

Key idea

A character that is grounded in a specific time and place is going to be a lot more real to you and your readers.

Consider the following:
- What are the physical aspects of your hero's home, both the house/apartment and the local landscape? Is it cold, hot, wet, windy? How does that inform and create his character?
- What are the cultural aspects of that place? Are there many cultures coming together, or just one? Is there an accent or set of beliefs that shape her?
- What are the spiritual aspects or feeling of that place? Does it feel isolated, suspicious, generous or kind? How is that going to influence your character?

Key idea

A great character has a goal but faces an obstacle or conflict. To discover the conflict (you always need a conflict because happy characters are boring), ask the characters these things:
- What do you want more than anything in the world? (*goal*)
- Why can't you have it? (*conflict*)
- What are you going to do to get it? (*the story*)

Write about your character's goal

Quickly write a paragraph about the goal, conflict and quest of your main character.

Embroidery: adding layers for fun

Pockets and pocketbooks

An old writing friend of mine, Alison Hart/Jennifer Greene, shared this trick with a group of writers many years ago. For a woman character, go through her purse and see what she's carrying around. How big is the purse, and what does it look like? If the character is a man, go through his glove box and his coat pockets. What did you find?

What is in your main character's purse or glove box? Set a timer for three minutes and write as fast as you can.

YOUR CHARACTERS' MUSICAL TASTES

Our musical tastes are a telling aspect of our personalities, and tend to be very specific. My 28-year-old son loves harsh, grating, loud, intense rock with heavy guitars. I love all sorts of music, but not jazz or country. It grates on my nerves. My eldest child, a serious sort with a serious job, is a guy who loves Taylor Swift.

A great trick is to find out what year your characters left high school and then run a search for the Top 40 hits in that year. It helps you to form not only an idea of your character's musical tastes (punk? soul? classic rock?) but also a spirit of the time when the character came to adulthood, which is a powerful influence on all of us. A character who came of age during the Nirvana years will have a different worldview from a character who came of age with Gwen Stefani.

Choose their music

What music do your characters like? What does it say about them?

RUNNING HOROSCOPES

This can be so much fun if you're stuck for details: figure out a birth date and go to the free sites on the Web and run the horoscope to see if you can get ideas to flesh out a troublesome character. This serves to remind me that no character is all good or all bad, and can give me some ideas to flesh out a cardboard character who is not doing any work in the plot.

Workshop: first-person autobiography

Sit down when you have a little time to yourself and get out your notebook. I like to put on some music that my character might like to listen to, though not everybody can think with music playing. You'll have to find out for yourself whether or not that works for you.

Set a timer for about ten minutes and do a timed writing exercise that you write from the point of view of your character. For example: 'My name is Jack and I'm an artist, returning to America on the *Titanic* after a stay in Paris, where I tried to join the art world.'

Remember the rules of timed writings: just keep the pencil moving and don't worry about what you're writing. The most amazing things might pop out about your character when you work this way! The idea is not to get perfect, polished words on the page that you can show off to everybody but to find out what your brain might have to give you about this character.

Write an autobiography for each of your two main protagonists. You can write autobiographies for all your characters if you wish.

Focus point

Great characters are memorable because they are specific, authentic and full of depth, and because we can relate to them.

Where to next?

In the next chapter, we will discuss how to create plots and subplots for these characters to move around in.

5

Plot and subplot

Of all of the questions I get about writing, most revolve around structure or, in other words, plot. Lack of good plot structure is also the biggest problem I see with beginners' manuscripts. The idea of a plot is not a particularly complicated one. A story has a beginning, a middle and an ending. We know this instinctively from watching a thousand television shows and reading hundreds of books. You have absorbed plot structure by osmosis; trust me.

In this chapter we will examine and experiment with several different plotting methods, including the hero's journey, the female journey, plotting for the right-brained, and Robert McKee's story values and the negation of the negation.

'The king died and then the queen died is a story. The king died, and then the queen died of grief is a plot.'

The basics of plot

The basics of plot can be described as follows:

1 Stories begin on the day things are different.

2 Something happens to sweep the character into a new reality, and she wants something (riches, accomplishment, love, marriage, children) very much.

3 An opposing force means that she doesn't have what she wants, so she must find ways to try to get it, but it is difficult and she encounters setbacks and trials.

4 It appears that all is lost.

5 The main character battles the opposing force and wins – or she loses, which would make the book a tragedy.

In most cases, romantic novels end on the up note, though of course there are many celebrated romantic tragedies. (One such book, *Me Before You*, by Jo Jo Moyes, has enjoyed tremendous popularity.)

Of course, this is how stories flow. You can feel it in your bones, can't you? We know it from early on in our lives. But how does this structure look in actual play?

 Key idea

You know the basic structure of a story from years of absorbing books, television shows and movies.

1 THE DAY THINGS ARE DIFFERENT

- Once upon a time a prince came upon a tower where a lonely girl had been locked away.
- Once upon a time a Montague went to a masked ball and spied a beautiful girl across the room.
- Once upon a time a very attractive man offered a chef the chance to create her own kitchen.

2 SOMETHING SWEEPS THE CHARACTER INTO A NEW REALITY

- The princess in the tower lets down her hair to let the prince climb up to her and they fall in love. The princess glimpses the possibility of freedom.
- Romeo creeps into a dark garden and calls out to Juliet on her balcony. They fall in love and want to be married.
- Elena Alvarez works with joy on her restaurant, which she opens even as she falls in love with Julian, her boss. She realizes she wants love and joy and happiness as much as everyone else.

3 A FORCE OPPOSES WHAT SHE WANTS

- The evil witch finds out that Rapunzel has been seeing the prince and puts a curse on her that condemns her to wander in the wilderness.
- Romeo and Juliet are married, but Romeo is then involved in a bloody sword fight and kills her cousin. He must flee the city.
- Elena and Julian become lovers, but she is haunted by her grief.

4 IT APPEARS THAT ALL IS LOST

- The prince is blinded and wanders in the wilderness. The lovers are parted.
- Romeo hears that Juliet is dead, and misses the message from the priest saying that she only seems to be dead.
- A second car accident forces Elena to face her fears and she leaves Julian and Aspen to return home.

5 THE CHARACTER FIGHTS AND WINS OR LOSES

- The prince and Rapunzel find each other in the wilderness. His blindness is cured and her hair grows back.
- Romeo kills himself at Juliet's side, and she wakes up, finds him dead and kills herself. The feuding families are united in their grief: 'A glooming peace this morning with it brings...'
- Elena journeys back to the site of the accident and makes peace with the incident that tore her life to pieces so many years before. She returns to Julian and they unite in love and understanding.

Key idea

There are ways to increase the cleverness and interest of your plot, but these are the basic steps: someone wants something, has to fight for it, almost loses, and then wins or loses.

Write about your plot

Write a paragraph of three sentences about the plot of your novel. Each sentence should answer each of the following questions:

- Who wants what?
- Why can't she have it?
- What is she going to do to get it?

Three ways to plot a novel

Traditional plot structure takes the form of 'the hero's journey', where the hero has to confront his own character as he overcomes the various challenges he faces during the course of the story. The plotline of 'the female journey' is similar, but with more focus on the struggle of a woman to find the strength within herself to become the person she wants to be and choose the life she wants. Plotting for the right-brained, or plotting from character, offers a more flexible way of looking at plotting, for those who prefer a less linear and less organized approach.

1 THE HERO'S JOURNEY

The traditional idea of a plot is a series of events outside the main character that force that character to confront something in himself. Classic stories are often based in what Joseph Campbell described as 'the hero's journey', with a clearly defined set of steps. That journey looks like this:

1 The ordinary world
2 The call to adventure
3 The refusal of the call
4 Meeting with the mentor
5 Crossing the threshold
6 Tests, allies and enemies
7 Approach

8 The ordeal

9 The reward

10 The road back

11 The resurrection

12 Return with the elixir.

This is a highly workable plot. Both Robert McKee in *Story* and Christopher Vogler in *The Writer's Journey* explore it in great depth. The focus of this model is on the male journey. Called to adventure from something outside himself, he battles to save the world (or the village or the girl) and then returns triumphant to the ordinary world. I've used it myself, most notably with *Heart of a Knight*. It worked very well, for one reason: *Heart of a Knight* is the story of the illegitimate child of a lord who has a chance to reinvent himself after plague decimates the countryside, meaning that no one knows who anyone else is. He dons a suit of armour and sets out to find his fortune, and follows his quest to better himself by learning what does and doesn't make a true knight. It is a classic male journey.

To structure a novel using this method, you will map the 12 high points listed above, and then fill in scenes between as necessary to add detail and bridges. How many scenes and chapters does your novel have? That depends on the number of pages, the sort of novel you are writing, and the pacing you want to create.

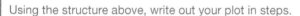

Write out your plot

Using the structure above, write out your plot in steps.

2 THE FEMALE JOURNEY

A romance novel is nearly always about a woman's journey, about her quest to find her mate and find herself along the way. To that end, I prefer the plotting methods described in Victoria Lynn Schmidt's *45 Master Characters*, which sets out a nine-step journey with a slightly different pattern from the hero's journey. A man is out to triumph and conquer evil, whereas a woman wants to find out how to survive and thrive, and then share that knowledge with other women.

The nine-step journey looks like this:

1 The illusion of a perfect world

2 The betrayal or realization

3 The awakening – preparing for the journey

4 The descent – passing the gates of judgement

5 The eye of the storm

6 Death – all is lost

7 Support

8 Rebirth – the moment of truth

9 Full circle – return to the perfect world.

As you see, there is some crossover with the hero's journey, particularly in the middle, but this method focuses much more on the community and the struggle of a woman to find the strength to become the person she wants to be, free to choose the life she wants and perhaps the man who will share it with her.

To structure a novel using this method, you will map the nine high points, and then fill in scenes between as necessary to add detail and bridges.

Rewrite your plot

Rewrite your plot using the nine-step journey. Which one feels more authentic to you?

3 PLOTTING FOR THE RIGHT-BRAINED

The maps above are very fine and well if you are a linear thinker, mathematical and neat. A friend of mine plots out her entire book in tiny squares on a single piece of paper so that she has the whole thing right there as she writes. I know others who plot with spreadsheets – which is perfectly logical, but makes me shudder.

I am not a particularly mathematical or left-brain sort of writer. There are several challenges:

- A book doesn't come to me in a linear fashion.
- I don't seem to like to know too much ahead of time, because it ruins the pleasure of telling the story.
- However, I do require a general structure to work with, one that is flexible but also provides some kind of girding to hold up the characters and ideas and themes and moods I'm working with.

As an experiment for Writer Unboxed, a writing blog to which I contribute a monthly column, I kept notes on my process for a novella I was about to write. As I did so, I realized that my plotting methods are designed for the severely right-brained; I am always holding the entire project loosely in my head, a collection of images and emotions and impressions.

Key idea

It feels to me that a story is a living, breathing thing. It exists somewhere, whole and beautiful and complete, and my job is to somehow draw it over into the physical realm as authentically as possible. To do so, I have created a system of worksheets and plotting rituals that are tools for brainstorming my organic process.

Step 1: brewing time

When I sit down actually to write a novel, it has nearly always been bubbling away on the back burners of my imagination for at least a year, sometimes longer. I usually begin with a character and a situation and, as time goes by, the book begins to pull itself together, using a snip of dialogue there, a beautiful room in a magazine, a sizzling steak, a piece of glass, a photograph, and often quite a few surprisingly concrete details, like a scarf or a dish or a gesture that is peculiar to one character. Eventually, scenes, themes and character arcs begin to emerge.

During the brewing period, I don't write anything down. If the characters, themes and ideas are strong enough, I'll remember them – it's a sort of natural selection in the world of ideas. (If I do a lot of research, I'll simply make notes about the materials I've read so I can find them again later.) I do sometimes gather images and tape them to a large piece of paper on the wall of my office, but nothing much more than that.

By the time I'm ready to start writing, I will know most of the story (albeit vaguely), the main characters, a few scenes including a strong opening image, a major conflict or opposing force, and a visual or a scene from near the end of the book. This is when it's time to start sketching out the story as it has assembled itself to this point.

Step 2: first sketch

When the book becomes insistent, I will sit down and sketch out, often by hand, a little bit of the story: the beginning, the middle and the end. For *The Lost Recipe for Happiness*, the book grew out of a single incident: there was one of those terrible accidents involving teenagers in my neighborhood, grisly and dramatic – five teens in the car and only one survived. It was on my walking route and I just could not stop thinking about the one girl who lived. What would her life be like after that? How would it shape her life?

By the time I sat down to sketch, probably a couple of years later, I had several images and ideas. I wanted to write about a woman chef making it in the male world of professional kitchens. I knew she had a dog. I knew she had a lingering injury from a car accident from which she was the lone survivor and that she would, eventually, have to make peace with her life. I knew I wanted to set it in Aspen (because… well, if you've ever been there, you'll know it is amazingly beautiful) and that my protagonist was from New Mexico because I am in love with the food and culture of northern New Mexico and wanted to write about it.

Step 3: character discovery

Because I am largely a character writer, my plots emerge from internal conflict. I often write bios in the first person, with lists of 25 things the characters love (more on this – voice – in Chapter 11) or conduct 'interviews' (see Chapter 4). When I get stuck, I often let the characters write letters to me, to tell me what's wrong. (India, the protagonist from *Lady Luck's Map of Vegas*, wrote, 'First of all, my name is so not Giselle.')

USING ARCHETYPES

This is when I'll pull out my stained, dog-eared copy of Victoria Lynn Schmidt's *45 Master Characters* and start playing with the lists of archetypes to help me pin down the corners of the book map. I write heavily from setting, so that needs to be established and solidified, especially as characters emerge from place. A Manhattan lawyer is not going to be the same character as a judge in Montana.

USING COLLAGE

Through this early stage, I will start building a collage, too. Results-oriented writers find collages a waste of time, but they help me discover images and themes. I need to find the colours of a book, which might seem like a strange little quirk, but it helps me understand the mood. Collages are also useful for brainstorming, and then, later, connecting myself back to the book if I get lost around Chapter 32. I can look at the photos and remember, 'Oh, yes. This is about sisters.'

Make a visual collage

Try making a visual collage of your work in progress, either using a computer program or with glue and paper and cut-up magazines.

Sometimes, letting go of the left brain means allowing room for the right brain to get to work and do some heavy lifting. You might give it a try.

Step 4: worksheets

I have a set of worksheets I've assembled from Vogler and Schmidt's books already mentioned and, once I've written 40–50 pages of my novel, I'll take some time to fill it out. If your inner school student likes worksheets, you can do this, too. Again, it's a brainstorming tool, a way to think about the material in an orderly fashion.

Most of my characters seem to be seeking to build a life that has meaning within the context of community, making sense of the shattering in their lives, so I use Schmidt's model fairly heavily. I also like her list of seven issues, examples of common problems characters grapple with, including facing fear, facing guilt and facing illusion.

Write about the seven issues

Consider the seven issues described in Victoria Lynn Schmidt's *45 Master Characters*, which are:

1 facing fear/finding security
2 facing guilt/expressing sexuality, knowing one's desires
3 facing shame, defining power and will, gaining identity
4 facing grief/accepting love and self
5 facing lies/communicating and expressing self
6 facing illusion/honouring intuition and imagination
7 facing attachment/finding self-awareness.

Which one (or more) of these is your character facing? Write it out and follow their journey.

Step 5: the synopsis and scene lists

Once I've filled in the worksheets, I have enough information to write a synopsis. This is required so that I can show my agent and publisher what I'm doing. If it were not required, I would probably skip this step. It is by far my least favourite part of the process. It often feels as if I'm rushing the development of things that I want to leave to discovery, but that's the reality: a synopsis is required for commercial fiction.

Key idea

A synopsis is simply a condensed version of the story, told in the present tense. You should be able to do one in about 10–15 pages. It is a summary of the story, giving an overview of the main idea, the main characters and all the turning points, the black moment when all seems lost and the resolution of the tale. This is told in narrative fashion, clearly and concisely.

From the synopsis, I write a rough list of scenes, just one or two sentences for each one, and only for the next 50–75 pages at a time. Or I'll write more than that and tell myself it's OK if it changes quite a bit.

Step 6: the principle of antagonism

Robert McKee

'The principle of antagonism: A protagonist and his story can only be as intellectually fascinating and emotionally compelling as the forces of antagonism make them.'

This step comes about midway through the book. I never know exactly when, but there will come a day when I feel suddenly lost. It's a long way from the start and that initial enthusiasm, but still a long way to the end.

This is when I pull out one of the geekiest books about writing of all time, *Story* by Robert McKee, and turn to the chapter called 'The Principle of Antagonism'. It deals with story values and themes and how to use their opposing and contradictory values to structure a novel. His diagram is a box divided into four squares, with the positive value in the top left corner. In the top right corner is the contrary value, below that is the contradictory value, and then my favourite part: the negation of the negation.

The negation of the negation is the darkest, lowest place the principal value can go. It's darker than hatred and darker than war. Using McKee's example:

Freedom	Restraint
Slavery perceived as freedom	Slavery

It's always easy to get the first three, for example to go from love to dislike to hatred. But what's the negation of the negation there? What's worse than hatred? It's hatred masquerading as love. Think about that for a moment. If you think you are loved, deeply, but it's only hatred masquerading as love, how deep is that betrayal? This idea lends tremendous power to a plot. If I know what my story values are and I take the black moment to the darkest place of all before the main characters learn their lessons and take themselves to that upbeat ending, it makes reading it so much more satisfying.

I also like this step because, by examining the current themes in my work in progress, I usually discover that I've not gone as deeply as I must to fully explore whatever idea I've presented. The novella I was writing when I observed this process dealt with the idea of having faith in things we can't see. The contrary is doubt. The opposing value is lack of belief. The negation of the negation is something like faith revealed as lies (which is why we revile hypocritical priests and pastors so much). Once I recognized that, I came up with a denouement that was much more powerful than the one I had originally planned.

Play with it. I notice that this one little exercise can do more for my plot than almost any other thing. Being aware of it helps me find the places to play up the corners of the chart and increase the tension and worry in my reader.

The negation of the negation

What are the values, positive and negative, in the book you are writing? Can you discover the negation of the negation?

Step 7: put it all away

Once this bit is done, I gather all my plot work, all my careful notes, and I put them away in a folder. I'll track my progress by keeping the simple scene list at hand, printing out a new copy every time I make big changes (and I usually just keep it open on the computer so that I can refer to it as necessary), but I rarely look at any of the rest again.

Workshop

Using the worksheets you've done on your novel using these methods, and the character autobiographies, write a five-to-ten page synopsis of your novel.

Include an introduction of your characters, their meeting and basic conflicts, combined with one of the above models of plotting.

Focus point

One of these plotting methods, or perhaps a combination of all three, will surely serve your process. One of the most beloved historical romance writers around, Jo Beverly, doesn't plot at all. She 'flies into the mist' and follows the story. Maybe that will be your method of plotting. If one method doesn't work, try another. Give yourself permission to do it in whatever way works best for you.

Where to next?

In the next chapter, we will look at how to orchestrate the emotional journey that your characters take towards the resolution of their story.

6

Orchestrating the emotional arc

At the heart of every romantic novel is an emotional journey, the journey of two people towards each other. That means that you have to understand how to reveal that journey in order to help your readers experience it.

At the most basic level, the plot of a romance is the story of two people who meet, fall in love, overcome their differences, and then resolve them for a happy ending, or fail to resolve them for a tragic ending. It sounds like the simplest of plots, but the variations it takes are as different as the journeys each of us have taken through our own relationships.

In this chapter, you will learn about orchestrating the emotional arc of the romantic story and its connection to the physical steps towards intimacy, and by using a number of exercises, find ways to get those ideas on to the page.

Julien Green

'The greatest explorer on this earth never takes voyages as long as those of the man who descends to the depth of his heart.'

The central story

Each of us is an individual, with our own quirks and desires and flaws. How we mesh, how we manage to get together and stay together in a relationship that supports and upholds us for (one hopes) a lifetime is endlessly fascinating. How do we know whether we have found The One; how do we know we have made the right choice? That's the central story, isn't it? If it were easy to be sure, there wouldn't be much point in romance novels. Fortunately for us, people are not computers and we have to go through a process of trial and error to understand other people, and to open up long enough to let them see us in return. It's an unfolding, often two steps forward and a giant step back.

A friend of mine, an author, will sometimes call me and say, 'Remind me again why characters do things that are against their best interests?' It's because of hope. It's because of despair. It's because of lust and longing and the whole raft of human issues and emotions. If your mother was aloof, you'll either be aloof yourself, fear aloofness, or worry about it in someone else. If you're aloof, how do you find connection with others and avoid the mistakes of your mother? If you are fearful of aloofness in others, what do you do if you fall in love with someone who reveals that flaw? Is it a deal breaker, or not? How do you grow into learning to love and understand that person, who is flawed just as you are?

It's easy to trot Ken and Barbie into a romance, both beautiful and smiling without many issues. They fall in love and live happily ever after because they are plastic, plastic, plastic. They're nice. They never snap at others when they feel stressed. They're always ready for sex or to have a great time. They never sit around the house in a pair of sweat pants, because they don't sweat. They are boring, boring, boring.

It is much more difficult – and, for a writer, rewarding – to write about fleshed-out, genuine, authentic characters who drag along their baggage and memories, their quirks and laughter, and then to put a couple of them together and see what happens. He loves her mouth but worries about her ability to earn money long term. She loves his laughter but worries that he's too lighthearted about everything.

This is where the emotion comes from, the push and pull, the longing and the antagonism of your two characters. They lean towards each other, bounce against each other and come apart, and then back together. It is in that sweet dance that our emotional journey lies.

Key idea

The bones of a romance novel can be described by a physical journey:

1 Meeting
2 Attraction
3 Conflict point 1
4 First touch
5 First kiss
6 Conflict point 2
7 Increasingly intimate touches (face, body, sexual parts)
8 Sex
9 Conflict point 3
10 Black moment
11 Happily ever after or tragic ending.

As a method of counting beats, it's quite a workable model, but it overlooks the key point: a romance novel plot is not about a physical journey but an emotional one. It is impossible to emphasize this point often enough. The classic understanding of a romance is that it's all about sex, the physical, and while that physical attraction is undeniably important, the journey is about the way we travel towards each other emotionally and create a lasting bond.

That said, the beats of the physical relationship often relate closely to the growing connection and intimacy between the two main characters. Let's examine those physical beats for the emotional underpinnings in each.

MEETING

The moment of meeting between hero and heroine is one of the most powerful in both of their lives. They may or may not realize it, but the reader does. In my historical romance *Lucien's Fall*, Madeline sees Lucien for the first time when he's having a reckless race with another lord, and Lucien takes far more chances than he should. Madeline does not care for rakes, for recklessness; she's a serious girl with a serious quest: to save her family land, most particularly the gardens.

And yet as he hangs there, he is undeniably beautiful and untameable, 'like Pan, like some untamed beast come in from the wild', and both the reader and Madeline are caught. While she rejects his recklessness, the reader is drawn in; for all that we want to dislike rakes, it is hard to resist a beautiful creature bent on self-destruction. The underlying message, one of the great tropes of romance novels, is 'I alone will be able to save him.' (Never mind the political correctness of such a scenario. Great stories don't care anything about political correctness. The tropes in romance work because we all have yearnings and programming and fantasies that have nothing to do with real life.)

Even as she resists her sneaking attraction, however, his recklessness makes something in her come alive. What would it be like to be the person who doesn't care, who can gamble everything on a single jump? 'To be so free!' she thinks.

There's the beginning of the emotional arc for the heroine. The hero's begins a little later.

 ## The first meeting

Write a few paragraphs about your characters' first meeting, from the point of view of the person who has the most to lose.

ATTRACTION

It is easy to depict the *physical* attraction between two people, and many writers are seduced into thinking that this is what the basis of attraction is all about. But beauty is easy – easy to describe, easy to capture – and, in the end, it means next to nothing.

What does matter is that moment of noticing that little something that catches us. The robust sound of laughter, rising above the noise of a party, signals – what? Is it enjoyment, lust for life or a lack of self-consciousness? Which traits are most interesting to your characters? Why will this character be particularly drawn to that one? Madeline needs more freedom, and Lucien represents it. He also represents ruin and she knows it; rakes are not reformable.

In Kinsale's *The Shadow and the Star,* Samuel Gerard is drawn to Leda Etoile on a level he barely recognizes. The conflict is centred very much around sex and physical attraction. Leda believes there is something wrong with her 'because her mother was French', and she has a strong physical response to the big, handsome, well-mannered and exotic Samuel. He, too, is bewildered by his physical feelings toward Leda, thanks to a childhood in which he was sexually abused by a man for a long time. Neither of them has any knowledge of how sex between a man and a woman proceeds (it is a Victorian story) but they find themselves coming together as if magnetized, while barely understanding anything of what they feel. Kinsale is a master of understatement, and worth studying for just that reason.

In the passage below, Samuel has been caught in her garret bedroom (he is an accomplished martial artist and has stolen something he hides in her room). The backstory is complicated, but Leda is leaving him to run for help, which would doom him. She forgets something and returns to the garret room, where she's just left the injured man a moment before:

> Her room was empty. She grabbed the door and peered behind it. The sword was gone. He was gone.
>
> [...]
>
> 'Broken leg indeed,' she muttered, lowering herself carefully back inside. 'Prevaricator! Horrid man!' She sat down on her bed and put her hands on her breast, letting out a deep sigh. 'Oh, thank the good Lord he's gone.'
>
> [...]
>
> Her mind went round and round with Mr Gerard. It was incredible. She must have dreamed it. She stretched out her bare legs, turning her toes this way and that. She thought she had rather pleasing ankles, trim and snow-white and refined. He would have seen them. She put her fingers over her mouth, flushing, and tucked her feet up under her gown with a bit more maidenly reserve.
>
> [...]
>
> She sat down with the gown rumpled around her waist. Her hair fell over her bare shoulders as she brushed it out with Miss Myrtle's silver brush, one hundred strokes on each side, trying to find some calm in the routine.
>
> But her mind skipped around in a distractingly foolish way, not concentrating on the problems at hand at all. She absentmindedly coiled up her hair and pinned it before she put on anything, stepped into her calico skirt, and buttoned her blouse, trying to use Miss Myrtle's hand mirror to see if anyone could tell she hadn't a stitch on beneath it.
>
> [...]

She picked up the mirror lovingly, turning it over and over in her hand. She stopped, and rotated it back half a turn, gazing down into the reflection. With a stifled shriek, she dropped the mirror and sprang back on the bed against the wall, staring upward. In the early morning shadow of the peaked ceiling, he lay along the attic beam like a panther, utterly still, watching her.

Laura Kinsale, The Shadow and the Star, Victorian Hearts (HarperCollins, Kindle edn, 2009), pp. 77–9

Everything is happening in Leda's mind. Another writer might have gone to Samuel's point of view to show us Leda's half-naked torso as she brushes her beautiful hair; instead we only learn much, much later how deeply Samuel was moved by that moment. It arouses him in a bewildering and powerful way that he must fight thereafter.

But the beauty of the scene is in the choice to stay with Leda, in her sweetness but also her attraction and her awakening awareness of herself. We enjoy the fine, quiet detail of her imagining that Samuel would have seen her ankle, never dreaming that he is watching her wash and seeing much, much more.

 ## Analyse the scene

Read through the scene quoted above and either highlight or write by hand the phrases that have allowed us to understand attraction.

 ## Develop your characters

Go back to the character sketches you created in Chapter 4. Come up with a dozen ways to illustrate why your characters are attracted to each other. For example, in *Titanic*, Rose and Jack are attracted physically, of course, but he is drawn to the soul she allows to slip out now and then, the soul of an adventurer, a woman of great passion who must be talked off a railing in her despair. She is drawn to his pluck and devil-may-care attitude and the adventures he's had. The woman with a sense of adventure is shown to us again and again as she poses nude, as she dances below decks, as she takes him into the hold to make love to him. He shows his pluck in talking her off the rail with jokes, and then by showing up at dinner in first class and refusing to be made to feel less than who he is.

CONFLICT POINT 1

'I am very attracted to you, but it would be a bad idea to get involved with you because...'

Each time the conflict comes around it grows greater and greater. Ideally, the conflict will be rooted in your values. For example, I have been writing a romantic series about a college-age group in which the main character is trying to learn to live on her own. So the values would be:

- independence/dependence
- helplessness/slavery masquerading as freedom.

Each time my character takes a step towards her own autonomy, the chance to revert to an earlier stage appears. Each time, the stakes are higher. That's conflict. She wants to be both in love and independent.

In *Lucien's Fall* Madeline wants the experience of freedom, but not at the cost of losing her gardens.

Helen Mirren

'There is that awful moment when you realize that you're falling in love. That should be the most joyful moment, and actually it's not. It's always a moment that's full of fear because you know, as night follows day, that the joy is going to rapidly be followed by some pain or other. All the angst of a relationship.'

FIRST TOUCH

We all follow a protocol when touching others. We might touch another person's arm in a friendly way, or link elbows. If two adults reach for each other's hands, however, it's a sign of attraction. It's quite an intimate touch. 'For saints have hands that pilgrims' hands

77

do touch', Juliet says to a smitten Romeo, and presses her palm to his, all that inner skin of her hand pressing into the moist inner flesh of his palm, fingers to wrist. 'And palm to palm is holy palmer's kiss.'

Write for one minute

Can you remember a time when someone held your hand and it was a moving, powerful experience? Do a one-minute timed writing on the prompt: 'I remember when ___ took my hand...'

Mae West

'Sex is emotion in motion.'

A wise romantic novelist takes the opportunity to make the most of each of these beats, telescoping the moments in the same way that you would feel in real life when you're in the midst of it. If you are very attracted to someone and he or she takes your hand, the moment takes on a gilded and sacred quality. The touch is new, and this hand is unlike any other hand in the world. What does it feel like? Is it rough or soft or engulfing? Can the touch, the moment, express something larger about what this relationship is or will become? Can you use it to foreshadow where the story will go, perhaps?

Look through the romances you've decided to take apart and find the moment when they first touch hands. What does it say? How long does the writing about that moment go on?

In *The Shadow and the Star*, Leda is a woman who is alone in the world and struggling to make ends meet without giving up her dignity. She has met Samuel in passing and now finds herself in quite an extraordinary situation with him. It is his hands that capture her attention:

> *...His fingers locked together in a twined steeple like a child's shadow game. She remembered his hands from the showroom: he'd picked up the silver scissors; rolled the bolts of fabric; held out the sealed envelope she'd dropped. A gentleman's hands, strong and well formed. She put her palms over her eyes...*

This is not a first touch of hands, but the passage illustrates how important hands can be in the progression of attraction.

FIRST KISS

The first kiss is one of the pinnacle moments in any romantic story. It is perhaps more important that any other connection, up to and including sex. A first kiss reveals and binds; it foreshadows what might come later in bed and how the two people will connect.

It is a sexual moment, but it is also a moment of intense emotional connection. Crossing the line of a kiss means that the relationship is progressing, is deepening, has more potential than was expected. It is often a moment of helplessness or bewilderment, or even surprise.

As with the first touch of hands, take some time here. Engage all five senses and the emotional heart of the story. Look for chances to reveal character, to bind the couple together as well as push them apart. It raises the tension to cross that line.

It doesn't have to be so much about the actual kiss as about what the kiss makes everyone feel. In *The Lost Recipe for Happiness*, chef Elena and her boss are engaged in another task when the bubbling attraction they have been trying to resist spills over:

'You okay?' he took her arm.
He was so close and she felt the dizziness of being so high,
and for one hot long second, what she really wanted was to
press her hand to his chest. Touch his tumbling black curls,
the fan of lines at the corners of his eyes.
The sultry tone of the music didn't help. He bent close, his
hand on her shoulder.
'I'm fine,' she said, breathlessly.
He kept looking at her face, and lightly pushed a lock
of her hair over her shoulder. Elena clung to the railing,
feeling a sense of being suspended in the air, as Julian's
eyes touched her mouth, her throat. She greedily devoured
details of his face, the way hair sprang away from his
temple, the skin so delicate that she could see veins
carrying blood to his brain and imagination. She admired
the arch of his dark brow and the moment was so strange
and high and out of time and space that she didn't even
think to move away when he took a step closer,
and then bent down, and—Kissed her.
Her first awareness was a burst of scent, something spicy
and dark, and she swayed under the force of it. His mouth

was wide, his lips deliciously lush and slow as he angled his head to fit their noses. She clung to the railings on either side, letting him put his hands on her face. He lifted his head for a blue second, their eyes meeting in confusion and permission, before he bent again, those heavy lashes falling, his hands on her jaw making her feel tiny and beloved.

It was too much, the flavor of him. He tasted of green water, a lazy lap of lips and tongue that made her breath catch and her back arch. Her breasts touched his chest.

It was such a vivid connection that the part of her brain that would have been screaming warnings was just awash in the green narcotic flood of him. And he, too, made a soft noise of surprise, taking a step closer to slide one arm around her waist. He supped of her lower lip, touched it with his thumb.

Suddenly she gathered herself, and pulled back. He didn't move away, but lifted his head. 'Wow,' he said hoarsely. 'Yeah, but no.' She swallowed, forcing herself to take a step backward, an action that made her dizzy. He saw that and stepped toward her, but she held up a hand. 'This would be just a terrible, terrible idea,' she said.

Barbara O'Neal, *The Lost Recipe for Happiness* (Bantam, 2008)

Notice in this passage how time slows down and how much detail is included. There is a lot of colour, black curls, a blue second, green water, green narcotic flood of him, and scent, and touch, and even sound of the music. They're high on a walkway, which adds to the sense of suspension and dizziness.

The reason this is so important is because it is a powerful moment of connection. Think about first kisses in your own life. Think particularly about a first kiss with a person who became very, very important, or one with someone you had ached to kiss for some time. Think about how many times you thought about it afterwards, reliving every single second, and all the emotions that washed up every time.

First kisses are wildly important markers. It's the moment a tentative relationship takes a step closer to something more. It's the moment you know you are definitely attracted to this person – or not. It is a very intimate sort of touch, full of things we don't share with just anyone, breath and flavours and smells.

CONFLICT POINT 2

Arising from the first kiss should be an increased level of conflict. Here, Elena knows she cannot get mixed up with the man who has all the power in her life. It's just crazy. He knows it, too, but is a lot more willing to go with it than she is.

Write for five minutes

Set a timer and write for five minutes about an important first kiss in you life. Write down everything you remember, in as much detail as you can muster.

INCREASINGLY INTIMATE TOUCHES

Depending on how much actual sex your book will contain or what sort of moral setting you've chosen to use, touching will escalate to include the intimacy of touching hair, faces and chests (breasts). Legs are intimate, particularly thighs. It can be quite intimate for lovers to touch each other's feet, as well.

As with other steps in this process, be sure you include an emotional component in each step. Think outside the box. How can you raise the tension between the two with these other touches? What prevents those touches from moving into sex? The dichotomy between wanting two things equally is what makes conflict interesting, in both life and books. Returning to the early example, the daughter of an aloof mother may struggle with the need to hide her emotions even as she wants to share them. A man who finds himself falling in love might both want sex and fear that he will fall over the edge with this particular woman (again the particular) if he lets himself indulge.

SEX

We will discuss sex in greater detail in Chapter 8. For the purposes of our emotional arc discussion, the important thing to remember is that sex should raise the conflict in some way. If you don't work out how to do this, the emotional tension of the book will fall completely flat at this point. (This is why television shows are so reluctant to let a couple actually get together – why then would the viewer tune in?)

Romeo and Juliet have one night together before he must flee the city, and they spend the dawn in tears of protest and resistance. She fears that something terrible will happen if he leaves, thus foreshadowing what will come.

One of the reasons I find *The Shadow and the Star* so compelling is the pinnacle scene of first sex between Samuel and Leda. He desperately wants to make love to her but he misunderstands some things about the situation – and about himself. She, too, misunderstands some aspects of what is going on between them; she's a virgin and has never been educated about the finer points. They are discovered and are forced to marry, which should have been everything Leda wanted – but it turns out not to be. It's a prison sentence, thanks to the masterly way Kinsale uses internal conflicts to advantage. It's impossible to include a snippet that conveys how powerful this scene is within the context of this book, so I highly recommend you read it.

CONFLICT POINT 3

As with Samuel and Leda, making love both increases the intensity of feeling between lovers and drives a wedge between them. Make sure that more conflict arises after first sex, or you'll lose the tension of the romance.

Analyse some love scenes

Look through your chosen books and read those first love scenes again. How is the author relieving and increasing the tension at the same time? What is gained and what is lost when the characters have sex?

BLACK MOMENT

When all appears to be lost, there should be an emotional black moment as well as a plot black moment. The lovers might still work together or feed each other, but it is critical that they believe at this moment that they have lost the relationship. It is not going to work out: whatever has come between them has rendered the relationship irreparable. Physically, this is when the intimacy that has been established is no longer possible. The characters are walled off from each other.

Key idea

In the black moment, it is crucial that the lovers (and the reader) believe that the relationship is lost and irreparable.

This is one of the most powerful events of the entire book, the place where everything you've built is cast into extreme doubt (which is why you must build a strong, believable conflict). Here is where you will use McKee's negation of the negation.

The negation of the negation

Look back to what you've written about the values in your book. What is the negation of the negation of your story values? Write down three things that might make it even worse for your characters.

HAPPILY EVER AFTER – OR TRAGIC ENDING

Romeo and Juliet are united in death and their families come to a glooming peace. Rose and Jack are reunited in death.

More often, the lovers solve their differences and find a way to be happy together. How have they resolved the emotional problems that divided them or kept them apart, and how can you show your reader that? Actions speak louder than words, remember, so never, never tell the reader that all is well. Show them!

Workshop

Write a step-by-step map for the emotional journey of your characters.

As an example, if I wrote the emotional journey for *The Lost Recipe for Happiness*, it would look something like this:

Meeting: Elena and Julian meet when he offers her a job. They are immediately attracted to each other – she likes his air of creativity and his black curls; he loves her plump mouth.

Conflict: he will be her boss, and will have no qualms about firing her.

Attraction: the attraction continues to build as they work together on creating a great restaurant and have a chance to learn more about each other. He is intrigued by her tragic past, and she loves his world, his calmness.

First kiss: is on the balcony. Increasing conflict is that she is haunted (literally) by the ghosts of her past, a past she has to let go if she is to live in the now. Another increase in conflict comes when writer Julian finds himself secretly using her story in a screenplay he's writing. He feels badly about it, but he's a writer – we're all guilty of using everything around us.

First sex: it is outrageously good and should not have happened, but the fact is, they are not turning back. Elena is coming alive, eating, drinking, having sex with him, and it's wonderful. (This is a very sexy book, though not erotic. Sex provides a metaphor for living, for life.)

Conflict: Julian is anxious that Elena will feel betrayed by his using her life story, and by the fact that she doesn't exactly fit into his very wealthy world.

Black moment (negation of the negation): this comes when an external event mimics the tragedy Elena knew as a teenager and she knows she has to make peace with it before she can really love another person.

Happily ever after: Julian offers her his screenplay so that he's not hiding anything. She returns to the scene of the tragedy, puts her ghosts to rest, returns to him, and they reunite.

 Edit your synopsis

Once you have written the emotional journey of your characters, go back to your synopsis and add these steps to it. How do the plot points and the emotional journey connect? Be sure to use the negation of the negation to cause grave doubt about the possibility that these two lovers can work things out. How can you add more conflict and punch – and eventually a better pay-off for the reader?

Focus point

When charting the emotional journey of a romantic story, be sure to keep the physical journey in mind, but remember that it is not the same thing. You cannot substitute the physical for the emotional.

Where to next?

Next, we will explore the profoundly important idea of setting and sense of place in romantic novels, an area often neglected.

7

Setting and sense of place

Readers of romantic fiction love to escape into worlds unlike their own. We love to immerse ourselves in moody English country houses or in the world of the small rural town. Readers love the Scottish Highlands and Welsh castles and the exotic sunny villages of Spain or Greece. It is much the same sort of escape as enjoyed by fantasy and science-fiction readers – running away into a landscape that is not *this* one.

In order to write compelling romantic fiction, you will need to understand and create powerful settings for your readers to slide into, and it's a sacred trust. The wrong details shatter the dream and your book will go hurtling across the room. In this chapter, you will learn how to build the elements of setting – geography, weather, culture and 'spirit' – to create a strong sense of place in your novel.

Pat Conroy, *The Prince of Tides*

'My wound is geography. It is also my anchorage, my port of call.'

The importance of setting

One of the most gripping books I've read recently was *One Last Look* by Susanna Moore. It's the story of an Englishwoman going to India in the 1830s, and her experiences there. What it's really about is her seduction – by India, which steals her heart, and we as readers fall right along with her. I've often longed to visit India, but this book made me positively ache with the desire to go there.
I even dreamed of India while I was reading it and, when I finished, I pressed it urgently into the hands of all the people I know who enjoy that kind of lush, perfumed sort of read.

Then, because I am not only a reader but also a writer, I went back through the book to see what had so captured me. What had this writer done so well? What I discovered is that India is one of the main characters of the story. It lives and breathes on nearly every page. I flipped through and through, and in every instance India is speaking, as the following quotation illustrates.

> *White Persian cats sprawled limply on the lawn, the tips of their tongue dripping from their mouths. Screens of white silk had been erected near a trellis of withered sweet peas for the native ladies who keep purdah... A young prince (girlish, scented, delicate), dressed in gold tissue and brocade and said to be the favourite of the Dowager Begum of Gharano, strolled back and forth, the toes of his curled slippers just visible in the parched grass, surreptitiously glancing at the girls as they struggled to tighten their bows.*
>
> Susanna Moore, *One Last Look*
> (Vintage, reprinted edn, 2004), p. 42

Can't you just smell it?

Bringing a setting alive

Think of a place you know very well and, as you read through the following discussions, consider what is particular about it and how you would describe various aspects of it to bring it alive to the reader.

In discussions of writing good romance novels, sense of place, or setting, seems often to be relegated to a place far down the list, behind things like characters and plot, dialogue, how to write a love scene or how to work in the science or the forensics. I teach at many writing conferences, but I don't often see a deep discussion of the subject of setting. Why is that? Do we take for granted that setting is something we'll get right instinctively?

I don't think so. I suspect that many writers think that place doesn't matter as much as character or plot, so it doesn't matter if we get it on the page as well as we do other things. As you might have guessed, I feel quite strongly that this is not true.

Rudolph Hinojosa-Smith

'Place is the spine of a writer.'

I would add to Rudolph Hinojosa-Smith's observation that the same is true of a great book: the place is the spine, the thing to which everything else is attached, and if we neglect the spine, a lot of the rest of the work will suffer. If you stop to think of almost any truly memorable piece of fiction, the setting is almost always so powerful that it's another character, and it's impossible to imagine the book sct anywhere else. Examples include:

- William Faulkner's *Light in August* (the south, specifically Mississippi)
- Larry McMurtry's *Lonesome Dove* (a cattle drive up the unsettled West).

This does not apply only to classics or literary novels, either. A strong sense of place elevates any work instantly. Think of the detective novels of Walter Mosley – the Los Angeles of the 1940s and 1950s is what gives them their zing, their flavour. Television has long known that place can be a big draw: we loved the first *CSI* TV show because the Las Vegas backdrop lent itself so well to the seamy crime drama. A precursor to that was *Miami Vice* and, before that, *Hawaii 5-0*. *Downton Abbey* would not work anywhere but the English countryside in the early twentieth century.

Think of movies. *The English Patient* is set in a very specific time and place: the Sahara at the start of the Second World War and a little villa in Italy after the war. Place permeates the film, with such luscious details that I highly recommend watching it with that single idea in mind. There is a discussion about the names for wind in the desert that prompted a discussion of wind on a writers' board I once frequented. I loved the way the desert dwellers were said to have taken up knives to make war on the wind. I posted the snippet, rapturously, and one of the writers responded, 'Oh, but I love the wind!'

It had never occurred to me that anyone, anywhere, liked the wind. Where I live, the wind will drive you mad in the springtime, gusting so hard that fences are blown over and you take your life in your hands to walk the dog. In the winter, it comes bearing sharp teeth to nip skin and ears. In the summer, it breathes fire and sets the fields and mountains aflame. That is my landscape. In my friend's world, the wind could be a breeze wafting through the trees. It could whisper and chuckle. Such are the details of setting.

Write about your world

Set a timer for ten minutes and write about your own world – not the setting of your book but the world you are living in now. What makes it special? What kind of weather do you have? How much sunshine? Keep your hand moving; don't edit as you go.

The three elements of setting

The three main elements of setting are:

1 **the physical**, which refers to the landscape, plants and animals: the geography
2 **the weather** and **climate**
3 **the cultural**, which refers to the groups of people who live in an area, their manners and morals, their language sets and accents, and the character types specific to that world.

1 THE PHYSICAL

Pat Conroy's famous novel *The Prince of Tides* begins with the words already quoted in this chapter, and continues:

> *I grew up slowly beside the tides and marches of Colleton; my arms were tawny and strong from working long days on the shrimp boat in the blazing South Carolina heat.*

The American South is the 'port of call' here and in a few words the author has given the reader a vivid image of that geography. Every landscape has its own flavour and the trick is to think about what it is. Every place is particular, and every place has set of stories it will best embrace.

My geography is the American West, specifically Colorado Springs, Colorado. I grew up with Pikes Peak, America's most famous mountain, at my shoulder every single minute of every single day; the string of blue curtains hung up over the horizon all the time.

Those mountains, my mountains, are the spine of everything I write. They are not the rolling hills found in some places, or the gentle foothills. They are mountains: craggy, harsh, most showing the timberline, which is at 11,000 feet.

Even if I change locations to some degree, shifting north or south or across the sea, I tend to find mountains to which I can attach my books. There's a good reason for that. I understand, on a gut level, how mountains react with the light. I know how sunlight and clouds move over mountains and into the valleys. I know, on a gut level, the influence that mountains have on people, and one of the most interesting is the fact that ignorance will kill you. No amount of charm, no amount of spin or fast talk will save you if you get stuck above the timberline and a lightning storm is on the way. You'd better be who you say you are, really know what you think you know, because what you don't know could kill you.

Think about the geography of your novel

The mountains and the sea are two very obvious kinds of landscape. What else is there? There are deserts, lakes, plains, hills… What is the geography of the landscape of your novel and how does that influence life in that place?

Flora and fauna

Describing the plants and animals in your landscape might seem like a fairly obvious idea, but it tends to be done from a negative rather than positive perspective: the writer wants to make sure that there are no obviously wrong things in the landscape.

For example, New Zealand has a truly exotic landscape. The geography of its mountains and hills could be transplanted to a lot of other places, but you always know you're in New Zealand when you look at the trees and plants. It's unlike anywhere else and feels like being on another planet, not just another continent.

When I visited, I understood that it was a very different world. The birds and the butterflies were exotic to me and everything was just *different*. I loved it, and I thought I understood the whole business of this delicate, isolated environment until I engaged in a discussion about possums, which had been farmed for their fur in the eighteenth century. When the market no longer supported the farmers, the animals were set free. Now they've become pests, and there are no predators.

I said, 'Well, you just need to bring in some coyotes. They'll take care of it.'

But then, of course, came the moment of illumination: there would be nothing to prey upon the coyotes.

That was my moment of dizziness – realizing that there were no large predators in those forests. There were no mountain lions, no coyotes, no wolves, no bears, nothing. (In fact, there is a terrible problem with cats for the same reason.) But here's the thing: I am very afraid of bears. There are many of them in the Colorado mountains, and I'm a hiker. I would love to hike where I never have to worry about them.

The remote biodiversity of New Zealand is an extreme example, but every environment is that specific. Use it to your advantage. Details are wonderful ways to pin the world down, to make it come alive for the reader.

Do your research

If you don't know the details, do your research. It is possible to get National Geographic videos on nearly every environment in the world. Watch movies set in your place; read books; find gardening almanacs from your setting. You'll quickly begin to understand the details you need.

Describe flora and fauna

What are the flora and fauna in your place? How can they be woven into your narrative to give a greater sense of verisimilitude?

2 WEATHER

In her sleep, Julia Robertson must have felt the change in the weather, for she pushed the blankets aside and brushed the thick blond hair away from her face. Occasionally Halifax has a winter day so mild that you could imagine the Gulf Stream, leaving North America for Europe, losing its way and creeping in closer on the coast of Nova Scotia. Then this severe northern province, like a hard-bitten spinster dreaming, receives an unexpected caress: hints of warmth borne north from the tropics, and false premonitions of spring.

Robert MacNeil, *Burden of Desire*
(Thomson Learning, 1998), p. 3

Every location has a particular climate, certain kinds of weather. Weather is great for establishing a mood, in obvious and not so obvious ways. The 'dark and stormy night' opener is a cliché for a reason. We can use weather backdrops to increase the particular atmosphere we want to convey, but we can also consider how weather might contribute to a culture.

For example, in Colorado, where the weather is sunny, light and nearly always fairly mild, people go outside. We live outside. Even in January, I can go hiking. I sit outside in the evenings all summer. Even in July, you can have a barbecue outside on a Sunday afternoon, and we do. We live outside – and that contributes to the culture in a thousand ways. Because the sunshine is so abundant, I grew up loving rain and fog and any other form of dark day.

By contrast, my husband was raised in the Weald of Kent, where it rains a considerable amount. The rain gives the landscape its trademark gardens and productive fields, but for a schoolboy waiting in misery for his lift home, rain dripping down his collar, it was not so lovely. In such a landscape, will there be as many outdoor activities? Because he grew up with so much rain, he loves the sunlight and I would never be able to prise him away from this sunny, dry place.

The effect of weather and climate on your characters

How does the weather and climate of your book's setting influence the people who live there? Are they expansive or reserved or straightforward? How do they dress?

3 CULTURE AND MILIEU

Every place has its own markers of culture, born of the landscape and history of a place.

My mother-in-law lived in a Kentish village where one of her neighbours and a group of other older residents walked every week along the public paths in the county to keep them open. One of them gave me a map, which I followed through the village of Hawkhurst and the surrounding fields, looping behind housing developments and along a stream and a bank of blooming purple rhododendron bushes. A white mare switched her tail beneath a single tree, surrounded by the open fields, and above the trees rose the towers of two ancient churches. I happened to know that one was abandoned and filled with fat pigeons, while the other sat on a village green, surrounded by a large churchyard with listing, mossy headstones, the dates worn away by time. I was stung by nettles for the first time in my life and took my life in my hands walking along the road where lorries and cars and irritable commuters zoomed by two inches from my body.

The people there are mostly white Englishmen and women with the odd Asian or Chinese person, or an African face now and again. These mostly white English people are from right there in the Weald, for generations upon generations back into a time that's so distant it's hard for an American to really grasp. I love that place, the village shops, the wellies on everyone's feet and the umbrellas at the ready. The locals made a national sport of the garden club and vied for the best prizes – the largest number of potatoes that could be grown in a container, the most astonishing wisteria, the best rose. They're kindly and a little aloof, and even I, with my untrained eye, can pick out social classes at 100 paces.

In contrast, I lived in Pueblo, Colorado, for two decades. It's a town on the open prairie 60 miles from the Rocky Mountains. The sun shines for more than 300 days every year and the annual rainfall is around 12 inches. The plants are prickly and pale – yuccas and sage and a broad selection of cacti. There are no stinging nettles, but beware goatheads, a thorn with a tiny bit of poison that will sink a half-inch into an unwary foot. There are rattlesnakes sleeping in the rocks and ranchers with sun-creased faces. It was settled by a mix of Sicilians and Mexicans, each bringing traditions and a heavy Catholic sensibility. It's a working-class city, based in a steel mill and the supporting industries. Family is the organizing principle of the city: marriage, children, grandchildren, cousins, aunts, uncles, extended in all directions. Everyone knows everyone and, if you need something like a plumber, you don't look in the phone book. You ask your friends until you find someone who has an uncle/cousin/sibling who does that kind of work.

Write about setting

Set a timer for 20 minutes and write everything you know about the setting of your novel. Don't stop; keep your hand moving.

As a writer, I am fascinated by both of these landscapes. Studying modern-day England has helped me understand how to write historical romances about it.

I first found my voice most solidly, however, when I wrote about Pueblo for the first time. The book came to me in a rush, all at once as I sat at a traffic light when I was driving a child to school. A local woman, Italian by background, brings her best friend back to Pueblo where he can die in peace.

I gave myself up to the rocking of the train, the endless, soothing sound of the wheels clunking over the tracks. I was tired. Scared. Michael and Shane had both made peace with the need and the reality of this upheaval in our lives, but I had a lot more baggage than they did. Roots. It wasn't just that I'd lived in the same house all my life, though I had. Same house, same neighborhood, same families that had known each other since forever. The whole group of them had immigrated from Sicily ninety years before. Two hundred families left a village in the southern reaches of that island, and transported themselves – lock, stock, and secret wine recipes – to America, plopping themselves down in a section of blocks in South Pueblo.

So it wasn't just a generation or two, it was hundreds of years of roots. Stories about things that happened before Napoleon was born, traditions that started in the sixteenth century, family feuds left over from 1742.

It only sounds romantic, trust me.

And yet, here is how it happened: the train came into La Junta at nine o'clock on a cloudy, late spring morning. We found the TNM&O station and got on a bus filled with migrant workers to ride the last little stretch into Pueblo, sixty miles or so. I took the window, my limbs heavy with remembrance as the potholed two-lane highway rushed under the bus. I spotted Pikes Peak, way off to the north, and the Sangre de Cristos to the south, blue and distant. They came closer as we trundled west, and a part of a Paul Simon song wound through my head:
'blood of Christ mountains...'

I'd forgotten how beautiful the yellow fields were in comparison to that soft blue of the mountains, how unbelievably huge the sky appeared. In my years away, I'd had a chance to visit Sicily and had immediately understood why my ancestors had settled in Pueblo. There were a lot of things that had the same feel, even now.

We passed through Rocky Ford, where the best cantaloupes in the world are grown, and I thought about eating piles of them when my mother bought them, five for a dollar, at roadside stands in August. We made ourselves sick on cantaloupe. I thought about telling Shane, but he was slumped deep in his seat, his hair hiding most of his face, and I didn't.

But when we got to The Lanes, I sat up and poked him. 'The house is right over that rise.' He roused himself, mouth slack, and nodded blearily.

Michael peered out the window, his hands folded easily across his lap, and showed not a flicker of emotion. He read a road sign. 'Ah, 32nd Lane. I get it, the Lanes, capital L.'

'Not all the names are that simple, so don't get cocky on me.'

He put a long slim hand on mine. 'You okay, kid?'

*'No. But there's nothing you can do about it.' I just had to
live through it somehow, these first few days.
Twenty years was a long time to be a runaway. It would
have been a lot easier to show up every
year or two in the meantime.*

Barbara Samuel, *No Place Like Home* (Ballantine Books, 2003)

Family, roots, local colour: I didn't deliberately set out to include those things, but I was writing about a world I knew intimately and all of those details showed up when I needed them, so I could make it live for the reader. That is what sense of place will do: anchor your reader in a particular time and place, and make the world seem real.

Key idea

Once you've done your research, set it aside and, as with a strong spice, use it judiciously. It can be difficult to resist pouring every single bit of your knowledge on to the page, but that can quickly become very boring for the reader.

I think of bougainvillea in the Harlequin Presents books I read about Spain as a teenager. I'd never seen it and didn't know what it was, exactly, but it sounded exotic and beautiful. It wound around the heroine's balcony. The hero kissed her beneath a nodding cluster of bright pink flowers. It was just enough to give me a flavour, a sense of what the world might be like if I were to open the door and find myself in that world.

We will learn more about how to select and use powerful details in Chapter 10.

Use the most powerful details

Look back at the writing you did on the setting of your book. Circle the most powerful details, the ones that represent your world most completely and consider how to include them in your manuscript.

Focus point

Setting is a powerful canvas for your book. Make sure that you do your research and get the powerful details into the setting.

Where to next?

In the next chapter we will tackle one of the most challenging areas of writing romantic fiction: sex.

8

Let's talk about sex

Ask the average man or woman on the street what a romantic novel is about and they will almost always answer: sex. It's one of the reasons romance novels continue to be seen by some as 'trashy', because our Puritan-based, religion-rooted society says that sex is meant only for procreation. We continue, even in this supposedly enlightened age, to carry around pockets full of guilt over the subject, even as we peek through our fingers at it whenever we get the chance.

In this chapter, we will discuss the awkward nature of writing sex, the fears and discomfort many of us have around the subject, and how to get around that in order to write sex scenes that are as competent and integral to the plot as any other scenes in the novel.

Gertrude Stein

'Literature – creative literature – unconcerned with sex, is inconceivable.'

The challenge of the sex scene

We have already established that romantic novels are not about sex. They are about connection and ending loneliness and finding a life-mate or a close companion to help us through a difficult time (high school, say, or the zombie apocalypse). But, as it happens, love often does lead to sex.

Of all aspects of writing romance, this is the one that is the most terrifying to many writers. How much should there be? How much is too much? How much is too little? How much detail should you go into? How do you know what to write? How will you be able to look your mother in the eye again after you've done it?

It is a highly charged subject, with good reason. Writing sex well takes as much thought, planning and skill as writing any other kind of scene. Unfortunately, our squeamishness or worry about what people will think of us keeps us from writing it well. Fiction abounds with examples of very badly written sex, sometimes so vague that one hardly knows what has gone on, or so incoherently flowery that it might as well be a Disney cartoon with birds and flowers and butterflies fluttering about, or so gracelessly graphic that it is embarrassing.

Write about sex scenes

Set a timer for ten minutes and write about your thoughts, misgivings, worries, excitement and everything else about writing sex scenes. What might get you into trouble? Who might be offended? What squeamishness do you notice in yourself, if any? What might be fun about writing sex? What would you like to say about it? What do you think about it, in general? Write it all down.

I have been writing sex scenes for decades, and it can still be challenging. The key is to be authentic and to structure the scenes in the same way you would structure any other scene: the scene needs to be there for a reason; it needs to advance the plot and raise the stakes of the conflict; it needs to reveal character or plot points.

There are other things that can help with the specifics of writing sex, ways to practise and get comfortable with it and decide how much heat you want and what is expected for the kind of book you are writing.

Writing great love scenes

To write great love and sex scenes, it's essential not to be squeamish, which may be easier said than done. Despite our conditioning, we must remember that sexual activity is normal and healthy and not a matter for shame or guilt. It's useful to read about sex in a scientific way, studying it as a biological process, as well as reading sex scenes as they are written in romances, to discover what works for you as a reader.

Key idea

Sex in romantic novels is about emotion, not biology.

Here is a step-by-step guide to writing great love and sex scenes.

1 DROP THE SQUEAMISHNESS

Squeamishness about writing sex stems mainly from a sense of shame or guilt. It isn't your fault if you feel that creeping sense of censure; our culture has pounded it into our brains and our churches into our hearts that we really shouldn't be thinking about sex, much less talking about it or – heaven forfend – writing about it! If we write about it, others might be titillated, might be driven to having more sex, and then all of moral culture will come tumbling down around our heads.

In fact, studies have shown that romance readers often do have more sex than their non-romance reading counterparts ('Women who read romance novels make love with their partners 74 per cent more often than women who don't,' according to *Psychology Today*). Rather than bringing the world crumbling down, my guess is that it makes their marriages and partnerships much stronger.

Key idea

Sex is natural, normal and healthy. It's also – dare I say it? – a lot of fun.

From a biological perspective, sex is the whole reason we are drawn to each other romantically. Every creature alive has sex, from fruit flies to gorillas to cats and birds. Humans bring a lot of complicated emotions to the feast, but we are as driven to have sex as we are to eat or drink water.

Sex is a natural, normal drive. In the right circumstances, it is enormously pleasurable and, between two people who are well matched and in love, it can be one of the better parts of ordinary life. That's part of its appeal, actually. We don't all have money or power or beauty, but most of us can find a decent, loving partner and have sex – even great sex. It's an accessible pleasure, like a great wine or a beautiful sunset.

But how do you deal with the fear of other people in your world reading your sex scenes? I won't lie: there may well be some awkward moments with people like your mother-in-law, work colleagues, the other mothers at the school gate or your husband's best friend. There will almost certainly be some leering neighbour you encounter. Someone in your family might disapprove and not be shy about telling you so.

My mother was once quite upset with me over the sex in *The Lost Recipe for Happiness*. She thought that there was too much of it, that it wasn't necessary. I think some of it embarrassed her, but I can't let the world come with me into my office and tell me what is acceptable to write. The book was about a chef who'd been grieving a terrible loss for 20 years. She opens a new restaurant in a new location, begins to fall in love, and then finds support to get over her losses. It's an enormously sensual book on every level. The setting is Aspen, which is an eye-splittingly beautiful place. Elena is developing recipes and tasting, tasting, tasting, cooking and serving food. And yes, there is a lot of sex with a very sexy restaurateur who has losses of his own to contend with. They are falling in love with each other and choosing to live.

On the other hand, a dear woman in my life, a devout, old-school Christian, said, when I warned her that there was sex in my novels, 'Child, where do you think I got those children of mine?'

Over time, you'll discover that, if you're writing something true and honest, something that feels right to you, it won't be at all uncomfortable, and people will respond positively to your lack of discomfort.

2 STUDY HUMAN SEXUALITY

One way to shed guilt and squeamishness is to learn about sex from a biological and physiological perspective. Study human sexuality and sexual behaviour by reading the *Karma Sutra* and Masters and Johnson. Study the function and form of sex and sexuality and you'll find your fears slipping away. Sex is endlessly interesting.

Depending on your setting, you might want to delve into sex in history as well. You will need to understand the moral imperatives of your chosen time period as well things like methods of birth control, disease and extramarital sex.

Study all of it – the negative aspects of sex as well as the happy aspects. As the singing duo Salt 'n Pepa urged us, 'Talk about all the good things and all the bad things.' The more you know, the more confidently you will be able to write.

Herman Hesse, from *Siddhartha*

So she thoroughly taught him that one cannot take pleasure without giving pleasure, and that every gesture, every caress, every touch, every glance, every last bit of the body has its secret, which brings happiness to the person who knows how to wake it. She taught him that after a celebration of love the lovers should not part without admiring each other, without being conquered or having conquered, so that neither is bleak or glutted or has the bad feeling of being used or misused.

3 STUDY SEX SCENES IN ROMANCE NOVELS

The way love scenes are written in romance novels varies tremendously, from very sweet to very graphic. To get a feeling for what kinds of love scene appeal to you, do a lot of reading. You may find that you want to close the bedroom door in your writing, or you might find the opposite to be true and that you love reading and writing about explicit sex.

It is more likely that, like most of us, you will discover that each book you write has its own requirements. One might need a lot of sex on the page. Others ask for something else. When I wrote *The Garden of Happy Endings*, I moved the actual love scene off the page because I knew there would be a lot of religious people picking it up. It is in no way an inspirational or Christian romance, but the main character is a minister who has lost her faith.

Write out a love scene

Find a love scene you have enjoyed reading and try typing it out.
This can be an excellent exercise in understanding sentence
length, breaks, pauses and word choice.

Sexual tension is the desire for more: a touch, a kiss, an embrace,
nakedness, sex. Once sex is achieved, the tension drops and must be
rebuilt. There is nothing more important about the emotional and
sexual arc of a romantic novel than sexual tension. Master it and
you will have readers eating out of your hands.

Key idea

Yearning is more powerful than satisfaction.

Laura Kinsale uses sexual tension in a masterly way, never more
so than in *The Shadow and the Star*. The hero, Samuel, was an
abused child and does not understand sex other than as a method
of punishment or a source of pain. He considers his love for a
secondary character to be pure and chaste and entirely appropriate
because he has no desire to kiss her or touch her in any carnal way.

Enter Leda, the heroine, for whom he finds he has entirely too many
carnal feelings. The sexual tension begins in earnest when he hides
in her bedroom and witnesses her bathing in the morning, her long
hair free, her upper torso bare. It's entirely modest, the whole scene,
but charged with a deep sexual tension, both from Samuel and then
Leda when she learns that she has been observed (see Chapter 6).

Leda, too, is innocent of sexual understanding. She is a Victorian
woman who doesn't even really know what's involved in sex. She
only knows that her mother is French and that must be why she
feels the stirrings Samuel arouses in her.

They are not in any way pursuing a relationship: she is his secretary
and a good one. He fully intends to marry the secondary character.

But when he returns from a business trip, Leda has been making
wine and is a little tipsy and more open in her gestures than she
would be ordinarily. Her slipping hair, his continuing denial of his
yearning, her soft rosiness and desire showing on her face and body,
combine to create a mood of moist hunger. He does not give in, but
tries to push her away. Her smell, her healthy hair and her shining
eyes all give him the most intense feelings.

He walks away.

Later, he tries a necklace on her, and touches her skin. She's nearly swooning with desire. He is so powerful, so restrained. She aches to kiss him.

Again, the desire is thwarted. They are in public; they are interrupted.

Later that night, he comes to her room and the relationship is consummated in a fiery, powerful, clumsy, intense union. But they are discovered, disastrously, in the morning. Both are shamed. Samuel is devastated that he will not be able to marry the other woman. Leda is devastated that she cannot win his love; still they are married and must travel on a ship to Hawaii.

The sexual tension again begins to build between them, now coloured with despair and love and loss. These two lost lovers must resolve the flaws and heal the scars of their own natures in order to find love with each other. It's quite a journey.

Thwart their desire

How can you thwart the satisfaction of your two lovers? What will get in the way of them consummating the relationship?

4 WRITE A SCENE LIKE ANY OTHER

Remember that a sex scene is a scene like any other in the book, and must have a point, must move the action forward, must cause more problems than it solves, and must have motivation and character development. Sex for the sake of sex is just boring. What do the lovers find out about each other, about the situation they are in? How can you raise the conflict? How can you satisfy and raise the tension all at once?

5 MATCH LEVEL OF DETAIL TO EROTIC INTENT

Some books in the romantic fiction genre are *about* sex. They are highly detailed depictions of sexual congress and include graphic descriptions of all aspects of sex. If you are intrigued by that kind of writing, there is an entire book in this series devoted to writing erotica and erotic romance.

Most of us, however, are writing on a scale of sexiness ranging from 'safe for children' to 'I might not feel comfortable reading this on the train.' Many things will influence this choice: the kind of romance you are writing, the line you write for (if it is category romance), the demands of the characters and the book itself. I tend to write at least one or two sex scenes in a novel but I have sometimes written many more or, in some cases, have chosen to skip a detailed depiction. In *The Garden of Happy Endings*, for example – a story about a woman minister struggling to come to terms with events both in her current life and in the past – I felt that Elsa herself would not want to get into too much detail about her love scene, so I left it out. However, there is still a heavy tone of yearning, of desire, in several of the scenes, especially a scene where she fries chicken that is then eaten by the two men who love her. Suggestion can be very powerful.

Details are where you'll make your choices, and you'll understand how much and where and how to include details by reading a lot of romantic sex scenes and deconstructing them, which you will do in the Workshop exercise in this chapter.

6 BUILD UP TO THE MOMENT OF TRANSCENDENCE

One of the most satisfying moments in a great romantic story is the moment when the lovers are transformed by their union. That happens during sex, and it can be transcendent and beautiful. We wait for that moment along with the characters, but it is not a physical journey. It is the emotional journey you plotted earlier. Set up each step and make us wait, make us wait, make us wait. Build that sexual tension until the reader cannot bear it for another minute... then orchestrate the union with great care. You will not be disappointed.

 Find ways to increase tension

Return to the emotional arc you plotted in Chapter 6. Can you find ways to increase the tension at each stage? Is there a physical journey you can connect to each of those moments, and details you can carry through in each scene for a major emotional pay-off at the love scene? (There is more on detail in Chapter 10.)

Workshop

Map the sex in three romance novels by asking these questions about them.

1 First touch
- What page?
- How much of a touch?

2 First kiss
- What page?
- How long is it?
- How much detail is there?

3 First sex scene
- What page?
- How long is it?
- How much detail is given?
- Is it consummated? If not, what interrupts it?
- How did you react to it?

4 More love scenes
- How many?
- How much detail is given?

Now write a sex scene (up to five pages) that might fit into your novel.

All of these tools should help you find your way through the sometimes disconcerting world of writing sex. Remember that we all want connection, that sex is natural and unbelievably ordinary – but it can also be transcendent, and when it is, it is one of the finest moments of connection two humans can share – or the most devastating.

Focus points

Here's a summary of how to write great love scenes:

1 Drop the squeamishness.

2 Read about sex in a scientific way. Study the biology.

3 Study sex scenes as they are written in romances. Discover what works for you as a reader.

4 Remember: sex in romantic novels is about emotion, not biology.

5 Remember that a sex scene is a scene like any other, and must have a point, must move the action forward, must cause more problems than it solves, and must have motivation and character development.

6 Keep the tension high until the resolution – the moment of transcendence for the lovers.

Where to next?

In the next chapter we will dig more deeply into the basics of how to write well, by understanding language, grammar, point of view and dialogue.

9

The tools of the novelist, part one

The entire goal of the novelist is to create what John Gardner calls 'the fictive dream'. I like to imagine this process as opening a door for a reader to step through, into another world. We are lucky in that the reader *wants* to step through that door. She is hoping with every hungry cell in her body to be transported. Who wants to read a mediocre book, or one with badly drawn characters or bad details? No one.

In this chapter, we'll discuss the basic cornerstones of good writing, and discuss point of view – first person, third person – and tense – past and present – and how to write good dialogue, including tags, and how to listen to conversations in order to write dialogue more authentically.

Steve Almond

'All readers come to fiction as willing accomplices to your lies. Such is the basic goodwill contract made the moment we pick up a work of fiction.'

Understanding the basics

We begin with an eager audience, one that is willing to be transported. Our entire goal is to create a world and people and a journey with such power that the reader genuinely feels she is living in another world. We have all had that experience of being so deeply immersed in a tale that we emerge into our own world a little bewildered, blinking at the bright light. Wasn't it just snowing?

Just as a carpenter has tools to build a sturdy house, the novelist has tools to build an exquisite dream for the reader. I've divided the tools of the novelist into two chapters: one on the basics and one on the finer points that will take your work from good to excellent. In this chapter we will deal with the basics:

- language and grammar
- point of view and tense
- dialogue.

LANGUAGE AND GRAMMAR

This topic is much too large to discuss in great detail here, and others have written about it more completely and with more expertise than I could ever hope to do. However, it must be stressed that language, all your words, are the most basic tools in your kit. The better you know your language, the better you can use it. In Chapter 10 I'll discuss how you can increase your language skills in ways that are enjoyable for most of us.

Every writer must take grammar and language seriously, even if they are using language for fun (and maybe then even more so!). If you haven't been at school for a while, or have never studied grammar seriously, it's a simple thing to brush up on. *The Transitive Vampire* by Karen Elizabeth Gordon is a grammar book that is fun to read and two excellent reference books on style are *The Chicago Manual of Style* and the *Oxford Manual of Style*.

Take the time to get it right. Look things up. If you don't know enough, take a quick brush-up course online or at a local evening class.

POINT OF VIEW AND TENSE

Point of view (POV) seems to cause confusion and misunderstanding among many new writers, so it is important to be clear about what it means. As with many things, it is not as complicated as it might sometimes seem. At its most basic level, point of view is simply the eyes through which your reader is experiencing the story at a given moment.

Key idea

These are the things you need to know about point of view for your story:

- Who tells the story? Is it the hero, the heroine, or both, plus others?
- It is in the first person or the third person?
- Is it in the past tense or the present tense?

You will establish point of view in the first paragraph of your book by giving your reader the viewpoint of the person she is going to experience through the book. The most common point of view for romances is the classic third person, and the past tense is the most common tense. Older romance novels sometimes used the omniscient narrator, in which a godlike view of all scenes and all characters is available to the reader. Modern readers prefer deep third person, where we are living *through* that character, in detail, as if we are that person.

Exceptions to this general rule are New Adult romances, which are often told in the first person and sometimes in the present tense. Young Adult romances are often told in the first person, too. Romantic women's fiction can use any or all of the above, according to the demands of the story. I have often used the first person in my novels, and have even used alternating first- and third-person points of view, so this is a flexible thing. However, because this can cause confusion for new writers, I highly recommend mastering one form before moving on to another or getting tricky in any way.

Write in the third person past tense

Write a paragraph in the third person past tense, for example, 'Ellen stepped outside to discover that it was raining.' Use the prompt, 'She parked the car at the bottom of the hill and looked up...'

Third person past tense is the traditional, accepted way of telling a story, and is therefore the easiest way for a writer to begin. Readers are also the most accepting of third-person narration. They're used to it, they like it, they understand it. It's also a structure that's easy to remember, simply because we are so aware of it:

> *Anna made her way down the hall in the dark. She winced when her skirt caught a statue of Pan near the library entrance and dragged it ever so slightly.*

Notice what changes if I change it to first person past tense:

> *I made my way down the hallway in the dark, and winced when my skirt caught a statue of Pan near the library entrance and dragged it ever so slightly.*

(A subtlety here: I changed the second example from two sentences to one because the repeat of 'I' at the start of a second sentence felt awkward. First person needs a somewhat different structure to avoid it sounding arrogant or repetitive.)

Now we switch to present tense:

> *I make my way down the hallway in the dark, wincing when my skirt catches a statue of Pan near the library and drags it ever so slightly.*

If you find yourself slipping in and out of the present tense, simply read the work aloud and you'll catch your mistakes. They become quite obvious when you speak the words out loud.

Choosing the best POV for your story

If third person brings such solid comfort for the reader, why bother to use anything else? The simple answer is that first person can be very compelling and can offer advantages that third person cannot.

First person offers the chance to immerse the reader deeply and immediately into a point of view, which means that the reader opens the book and becomes the character. Everything that happens is happening to the reader in a more visceral and more sympathetic way: we feel that *we* are the protagonist of the story. This means that, if there is something unattractive about the character or some other thing that needs to be slightly hidden until a later point in the book, it can sometimes be easier to create sympathy for a character in the first person. For that reason, a character with a secret is best managed via first person. (*Gone Girl*, by Gillian Flynn, makes brilliant use of the justifications we use, and it works because it's in the first person.)

I had written 20 or so romances in the third person past tense when I realized that the character arriving on screen for *No Place Like Home* kept telling her story in the first person. I resisted for quite some time, writing several chapters in the classic third person. But I was struggling and finally decided to switch to first person. What was the worst that could happen? I'd write a few chapters and realize that that didn't work either. No big deal.

The main character in that book, Jewel, has a chequered past and is not apologetic about it. I worried that my core romance readers would not find her sympathetic, so I rolled the dice and chose to bring the reader into the story on a very deep level, to allow them to experience *being* Jewel, with her beloved but rebellious teenage son Shane and her dying best friend, when she returns to her home town after 17 years.

Let's follow straight on from the excerpt from *No Place Like Home* that I used earlier to illustrate sense of place, and notice how, as we read in the first person *as* Jewel, we live with her nerves and we are inside the moment when she realizes that her sister has arranged a surprise welcome.

And it wasn't like I'd been incommunicado. It wasn't that dramatic. When my sisters Jordan and Jasmine, one year and two years younger than me respectively, got out of the house, we set up friendly lines. My mother got over wanting to kill me for dropping out of school within a couple of months, and told me to call her every Tuesday night from then on. Tuesday is my dad's bowling night. My father, on the other hand, has not spoken to me one time in twenty years, but I can't say I didn't know it would be that way. I did.

The city arrived outside the windows, so much bigger than it had been that I was blinking. 'Shane.' I said. 'Time to wake up. We're almost there.'

My sister was going to meet us and drive us out to the house. My sister Jordan, that is, the only one I'd told I was coming, the only one, in all honesty, that I was absolutely sure would come to get us. As we pulled into the station, I sat up tall, straining for a glimpse of her. The bus rocked side to side like a lumbering elephant entering the driveway.

We came around the corner and there they were. I don't know how many. Twenty or thirty at least – my sisters and their families, some of my cousins and aunties, and my mother, standing anxiously at the front. Someone had made a big sign that said, 'Welcome home, Jewel and Shane' with five exclamation points.

Shane said, 'Are they for us?'

'Yeah.' That was the thing I'd forgotten to tell them about roots, the upside. Even when you totally screw up, your sister will organize a giant surprise welcome for you. She'll be wearing a medieval velvet hat she bought at the Renaissance Festival, and she'll have put on a dress for the first time in five years, even though she lives in clay-stained jeans or surgical blues.

I saw her standing there, and waited until I caught her eye, then put my hand on the window, palm out. She raised her hand. Both of us had tears running down our faces.

Then I was up and running down the aisle. They spotted me and everybody started cheering. All of them, I swear, surged forward, arms out to enfold me, touch my head and exclaim and kiss my cheek. They blurred together in their clean shirts and good haircuts and the solid shoes of the old women, and the rosary in my Nana Lucy's hand. She felt like sticks when I hugged her, and all at once I was dizzy with the recognition that she was still alive. How could I have dared let so much time go by?

My father wasn't there. I hadn't realized until then that I'd been harboring some hope that he might be ready to throw in the punishment towel.

At last, everybody kind of cleared away, or maybe they surged around Shane. Either way, I was just standing there, looking at my mother, who also had big fat tears rolling down her pretty face. 'Finally,' she said, and hugged me.

Barbara Samuel, *No Place Like Home* (Ballantine Books, 2003)

So, before we learn that Jewel ran away from home at the age of 17 on the back of a motorcycle and bore a child out of wedlock, before we find out about all of her misadventures and multiple lovers, we learn that she loves her family and misses them and is doing the right thing for her beloved, dying best friend.

Rewrite in first from third person

Find a piece of writing in the third person and rewrite it in the first person. It can be your own writing or a passage from one of the novels you are studying.

First person is a workhorse. It helps establish voice and character with a cadence all its own. We hear the voice of the character the way we would the voice of a friend. It is also a more modern way to tell stories, and immediately establishes that this is not a classic romance. It helps set the ground rules: people may die in the book; this might be a grittier story. That is partly what it signals in New Adult, for example. In YA, the first-person voice helps with reader identification.

Change the POV and tense

Take the Snapshot you wrote in the third person past tense and rewrite it into first person present tense. Read it aloud to make sure that you stayed within the same POV and tense throughout.

The effect of POV and tense

What do you notice about the way these different points of view shoulder the story? What feels right for your work in progress? What might change if you experiment with another point of view or tense?

Changing POV: head-hopping

The rules of point of view are quite strict: change point of view only when you have reached a scene break or chapter break – and only then. If you are moving from hero to heroine, wait until the end of the scene to make the break. Any other way is a violation of the way we naturally read (and think).

You will see many examples of writers disregarding this rule. It was once done in omniscient point of view (the godlike view) but that's an old-fashioned form of storytelling and generally frowned upon now.

At times, you will be tempted to 'head-hop'. In my earliest books, I was imitating an omniscient point of view and head-hopped merrily, but there are two things it does wrong: it undercuts the tension of a scene, especially when the stakes are emotional; and it also jars the reader out of what John Gardner calls 'the fictive dream'.

Key idea

Change point of view only when you have reached a scene or chapter break – and only then.

Dialogue

Nicholas Cage

'When I act, I hear it like music. In my head, I hear the dialogue like music.'

Dialogue is a subject that gives many aspiring writers a headache. They worry about where to break the dialogue, how to insert tags and how to make it flow easily and naturally.

Again, we tend to make this much harder than it actually is. It's harder to talk about dialogue and think about dialogue than it is to actually write it. What could possibly be more natural than to write down conversations? We've all had zillions of them. We know how they flow, what they should sound like. Trust your ear. You have been talking all your life and listening to other people talk, too. You know in your gut what sounds right and wrong, especially if your character shares your background. Oh, she doesn't? Well, that makes it a little more challenging.

Most of your characters probably won't speak in the same way as you. The way you learn to make them sound authentic is by listening attentively to the people who talk around you all day long, every day. Pay attention and gather details. I've successfully given an exercise to my voice students for over a decade, described below, which involves deliberate eavesdropping in order to hear how people actually talk. Once you begin to really listen, you'll hear the natural beats of pausing and emphasis that are so much a part of how we speak. Body language, too, is a powerful method of communication and is part of our repertoire as writers.

What about the flow of conversation on the page, the nuts and bolts of recording a conversation that reads naturally and easily? We don't write exactly the way people talk. In real conversation, we interrupt and talk over each other; we break off and think, we ramble around to the point. In a novel, dialogue has to have a point, a reason for being included, so it can't ramble around.

In dialogue, exchanges tend to be shorter than in real life, and we use tags ('he said', 'she asked') to create rhythm and flow, just as we would with other parts of writing. The use of body language also gives a strong sense of emotion on the page, as in this example from *The Shadow and the Star* by Laura Kinsale. The time period is the Victorian era, the setting England.

Leda's heart began to pound with greater terror than before. That he could kill her if he pleased she had not the slightest doubt; there was not one trace of humanity or compassion in his perfect face, not a shadow of mercy. She began to feel ill again.

'Think of the water falling,' he commanded softly.

She swallowed and let the air flow from her lungs, still staring at him.

'Try to calm yourself,' he said. 'I'm not going to murder you. Tonight my—composure—seems to elude me. I didn't intend you any hurt.'

'This is utterly insane,' she said weakly. 'Why are you in my room?'

'I'm presently in your room because you have broken my leg, Miss Etoile.'

'Broken your...but I...oh, mercy!'

'It's something of an inconvenience, yes.'

'Broken your leg,' she repeated in despair. 'But surely not! You were standing a moment ago!'

'With some concentration,' he said. 'The agent of my undoing would seem to be a sewing machine.' He looked at the fallen contraption and added enigmatically, 'Perhaps I should find some enlightenment in that.'

She curled her fingers in her nightgown, frowning at his outstretched leg.

Laura Kinsale, *The Shadow and the Star, Victorian Hearts* (HarperCollins, Kindle edn, 2009), pp. 77–9

Notice that the conversation flows very naturally and you can hear the intonation and formality of the British English of the Victorian period. It is easy to pick out the differences between the speakers, almost hearing the softer, deeper tone of Samuel's voice, the less sure voice of Leda. Notice how the tags are used to give rhythm and cadence to the flow, and they are not always at the start or the middle or the end. They are also not all 'said', but often describe an action, which keeps the dialogue feeling lively.

Notice tags

Go to one of the books you are studying and find a longish passage of dialogue. Notice how the writer uses tags. Are there many of them, or only a few? Does the writer use any other tags besides the very common 'said' and 'asked'? Is there a lot of action? How is it included in the speeches? Does it feel natural to you? Can you hear the differences in the speakers? How?

Tags are a tricky proposition. One of my journalism professors used to say to us, 'There are 200 synonyms for "said" in the English language. Don't use them!' For the most part, this is an excellent rule of thumb. 'Asked', 'told', 'whispered', 'shouted' are all fine now and then, but stay away from the more colourful terms or, if you must use them, do it as sparingly as you would wear neon orange. Those words call attention to themselves, which means that the dialogue ceases to be a window into the story and suddenly proclaims itself to be *writing*. That's exactly what you don't want.

Good dialogue is a powerful part of your story and it is something that must be mastered through practice. It helps keep the narrative active, and will pick up the pace of a flagging scene. If dialogue is written with verve and with attention to moving things along, showing us more of the story, it can make the writing feel much faster paced. We read dialogue more quickly, or at least it feels that way, when we see all the white space.

Avoid 'as you know' constructions. 'As you know, Jake,' one character says to another, 'we have been following this case for five years.' Again, it pulls the reader out of the story and never feels natural.

Read your dialogue aloud for cadence and finding the beats. It will help you pick out the stilted phrases, the unnatural breaks and tags, and give you a sense of what you're really getting on the page. Better still, read it aloud to someone else.

Workshop

Go somewhere where you will be able to listen to conversations easily, perhaps a local restaurant or a bus station, a pub or café. Take a notebook and do your best to write down exactly what you hear.

- Who are the people talking?
- Can you tell their social class and what standing they have from their language?
- Is there an accent?
- Are there power dynamics?

Do this exercise for five minutes a week until you begin to do it automatically whenever you're standing in line or whenever you might have to sit alone in a public space like an airport or restaurant. Listen to your family and friends, too, and pay attention to how you know when someone is signalling a particular emotion. Does their voice rise? Are their words clipped? What kind of body language signals are you picking up? How do you judge the sound of social class? Is it by accent or intonation?

Focus points

Third person past tense is the most common point-of-view and tense choice for romantic novels. In second place is first person past tense.

First person enables the reader to become much more deeply immersed in a character's mind than the third person. That is why it works so well in some instances, and also why some readers don't like it: it feels too intimate for many.

Dialogue in a novel is not there just for the sake of filling space: it has to have a point, a reason for being included, so each piece of speech must have a purpose; it can't ramble as it would in real life.

In the next chapter we will deal with more of the tools of the novelist – the elements that can make the difference between good writing and great writing.

10

The tools of the novelist, part two

Once you've mastered the basics of language, point of view, tense and dialogue outlined in the previous chapter, you're ready to move on to the cornerstones of excellence, evoking all five senses to bring your work alive for your reader. By mastering the art of the telling detail and by adding small beauties of motif and grace notes, you will take the emotional satisfaction a reader gains from your story from good to great.

In this chapter, we will discuss and try out some of the more elegant tricks available to us, and learn how to use them. We will talk about how to use the five senses, and how to use the telling detail for maximum impact. Finally, we'll touch on grace notes and flourishes.

Gordon B. Hinckley

'Mediocrity will never do. You are capable of something better.'

Taking your writing from good to great

What is the difference between a good cook and a great one? A good cook knows ingredients and can follow recipes and is able to produce tasty meals. A great cook, however...

- will taste a dish and run through all the possibilities to discover the two or three herbs or spices that will elevate the flavour and make the dish sing
- is not afraid to experiment – she knows that a brilliant failure still teaches her something
- knows that the diner really wants to love what she presents, but also knows that great presentation adds to the depth of pleasure of anticipation and eating the dish.

In the same way, a great writer knows:

- how to use all the tools available to create a world that feels absolutely real
- that all five senses matter
- how to use colour
- how to use and manipulate setting and tone
- how to listen to the word choices and sentence rhythms of a piece to help create the effect she wants to create.

How do you gain mastery of all these tools? Some of it is a matter of being born with a great eye or a great ear or a terrific understanding of the flow of things, but every writer can learn to be a great listener and a great observer.

CLEARING AWAY MISCONCEPTIONS

This chapter is an overview – maybe a refresher course for some of you – of time-honoured techniques writers have been using for a long time to make writing live and breathe and deliver a deeply satisfying reading experience. However, there are some common misconceptions about what excellence means:

- Excellence is not about being a poetic writer. Certainly, if that's your bent, go for it, but that is not what I mean by elevating your writing. When I talk about mood, I don't mean 'moody'; I mean tone and spirit. What is the tone and spirit of this work? When I say atmosphere, I'm not talking about a ghost story kind of feeling or the brooding mood of 'a dark and stormy night'. It is about detail work and word choice and the whole 'geeky' level of writing that a lot of people give up on.
- It is *not* about how to write really long descriptions of everything from the sunrise to the lace on the hero's sleeve. It is about how to elevate your writing with techniques you might have forgotten about: things such as onomatopoeia and cadence and how to key into the five senses – yours and your reader's.
- It is *not* a plea to return to the Victorian tomb of boring and more boring. There's a reason they wrote such long books: it gave everyone something to do on those long evenings before television or the computer. We, on the other hand, are competing with those instant, sparkling media so we'd better be able to deliver honest-to-God entertainment – or at least really good thinking material.

Most of the techniques outlined here will be used after you have completed a rough draft and are ready to begin polishing the material. It's a lot easier to layer in richness once you know what you're working with. I'll break down the process a little later, but let's start with some exercises and discussion first. I'm also going to include some readings.

Write for one minute

Set a timer for one minute and get out your notebook. Write for one minute, using the prompt: 'In this moment, I am…'

BECOMING AN OBSERVER AND A NOTE-TAKER

Great writing is about becoming an observer and a note-taker. It means paying attention to everything, the way things look and taste and feel and smell and sound – and storing that away, constantly, like a little computer. Mostly we are so busy that we don't pay attention to the very moment we're living in. We're off in the future, worrying about everything that has to get done, or off in the past, worrying about things that should have gone a different way or things we'd change if we could, or – whatever.

You can observe things right now, this very instant. You can hear things, taste things, feel things. Your shoe might be pinching or your shoulder blade itching or you might feel the edge of your contact lens scraping against the edge of your eye.

Write for another minute

Now go back to your notebook and write for another minute on 'In this moment, I am…' Keep it in the present. Make it concrete. Notice everything you can and record it – this very moment that will never be here again.

I began using the 'In this moment…' prompt as a way of keeping a journal when I travelled. The point of travel is to be where you are, experiencing what is new and different and strange, but it can be easy to be distracted by discomfort or homesickness or any number of other things. By writing about this moment, I am present with the adventure and more fully cement my memories.

Here's one I wrote on a Venice Beach afternoon in April:

> *In this moment, I am sitting on Venice Beach. A soft wet breeze is filling my dry pores. The sun is burning my left shin. I am quiet inside. The ocean stills me with all its noise and motion. I want to go to sleep.*

Using all five senses

List your favourite things

Write the numbers 1 to 25 on a sheet of paper. Set a timer for six minutes. Write a list of things you love. They could be anything: humans, animals, weather, clothing, foods, whatever you want, but they have to be things you really, really love. Just don't write the name of the thing, but include a brief description (e.g. 'rough-haired dogs').

One thing: don't name your spouse and children. It's OK to name something you like about them, but just putting them on the list isn't going to help with this exercise.

When you have finished, take a few moments to see whether you can pick out a primary sense. If your list has a lot of food and descriptions of wine and meals, taste is your main sense. If everything is described by its colour, you are a mainly visual person. We all have one or two senses that are stronger than others. What do you notice about *your* list?

If we go through those senses one at a time to see how they can be used, we will see that they are all essential elements of great writing.

SIGHT

Sight is what we use to create the visual setting in a novel. We tell the reader what she is looking at, whether it is blue sky and trees in a trimmed green park or a crowded club late at night, smoky and grim. Visual details are often the easiest for writers to begin using.

This is where description falls, and you know to be careful with it. We don't need long, drawn-out visual descriptions of a room, for example. What's more, we don't even see that way. When we walk into a room, we notice only certain things, things that don't fit the big picture, and maybe a detail or two.

The trouble with a lot of description is that it has no emotional shading. As writers, we need to point out the details that matter to the story.

Here is a description of a room:

> *The living room was a plain ranch style from the '70s. The walls were white, the front window a big square. There was a couch and chair covered in rose chintz with piles of multi-coloured pillows, and two end tables with lamps, and a corner cabinet with a collection of glass prettily displayed. Magazines neatly spread in a fan covered the coffee table.*

Compare that description to this one:

> *The living room was a classic 70s monolith – a bald rectangle with a boring picture window and absolutely zero charm. But even here, Tom could see Sarah's quirky stamp – the vintage martini glasses and ceramic pink lamps that matched the neon pillows on the flowered couch. She'd ripped out the grimy old shag carpet and raised the ceilings. The magazines on the table were vintage Better Homes and Gardens with pineapple spam recipes on the cover. He smiled. His sister always did have a sense of humour.*

In other words, the details should tell us something.

Anton Chekhov

'Don't tell me the moon is shining; show me the glint of light on broken glass.'

An example of how word choices build a visual picture is this excerpt from *One Last Look*, a novel we looked at earlier:

> *White Persian cats sprawled limply on the lawn, the tips of their tongue dripping from their mouths. Screens of white silk had been erected near a trellis of withered sweet peas for the native ladies who keep purdah... A young prince (girlish, scented, delicate), dressed in gold tissue and brocade and said to be the favourite of the Dowager Begum of Gharano, strolled back and forth, the toes of his curled slippers just visible in the parched grass, surreptitiously glancing at the girls as they struggled to tighten their bows.'*
>
> Susanna Moore, *One Last Look*
> (Vintage, reprinted edn, 2004), p. 42

What saves this from being purple prose?

- It's a literary novel.
- It's about India and the lushness of the sensual setting that steals away the main character.
- The word choices (discussed below) underline the lusciousness of that particular setting.

 ## Booker T. Washington

'Excellence is to do a common thing in an uncommon way.'

Colour

When I was about six years old, my teacher wrote the names of the colours on squares of paper and hung them up around the classroom. I can still see them in my imagination, the orange square with the word 'orange' on it. It seemed so powerful to me to know how to write those words down, to *claim* them.

You may remember those big boxes of school crayons with their evocative names, such as:

- burnt sienna
- periwinkle
- orchid
- cerulean
- magenta
- cornflower.

Think of colours you love, the names of them. Let them just play in your head for a minute. Doesn't that just feel luscious?

Not long ago, I was on a plane over the American Southwest at sunset, and the colour of the sun was so intense, bleeding all over the skies, that I just kept trying out names to describe it. It was more than orange, less than scarlet, touched with yellow but not really that at all. Then vermilion popped into my mind. Yes: vermilion. How's that for a great colour word? Vermilion skies.

I love colour. It is probably a result of my love of gardening or photography – or perhaps I love those things because I love colour, but I know a book is going to be a book when I get the colours of it. *Lady Luck's Map of Vegas* was silver and turquoise with splashes of red. *The Lost Recipe for Happiness* was painted with the pink and orange palette of *el Día de los Muertos*, the Day of the Dead.

How does this make a book better? Why would you want to bother with it?

Colour is what defines and illuminates our world. It lights up every single thing it touches, and it has a great bearing on tone and mood in writing. Consider the difference between a grey sky, a gunmetal sky and a purple sky. Consider what is conveyed by whether a woman chooses a white evening dress or a red one or something in navy blue. Colour has meaning and associations for us, and because of that, it can be a shorthand way of showing instead of telling.

Georgia O'Keefe

'I found I could say things with colour and shapes that I couldn't say any other way – things I had no words for.'

Choosing colours to represent the book can be grounding for the reader – and for you as a writer – and bring the focus back to your main idea. For example, in *The Lost Recipe for Happiness,* I initially wrote that when the protagonist first sees the man who is going to change her life he's wearing a turquoise scarf. It's a very minor detail but, when I went back through the manuscript, I realized that the colour didn't fit with the colours of the book, which are orange and pink for the Day of the Dead. So instead I gave him an orange scarf just faintly touched with pink stripes. It's the first view of this character, and that subtle, controlling image helps immediately to ground the reader in the world of the story.

SOUND

How do you get music or poetry on to the page? You pay attention to the sound of the words as they hit the page. Words have rhythm, pace and cadence. Some words are crisper than others – or sharper, softer or warmer. Some consonants clatter, some hiss, some hum.

Let's go back to that piece by Susanna Moore: notice now the alliteration. Read it aloud and you will see what I mean.

The language creates the mood; the word choices create the mood. Reading poetry is a great way to sensitize yourself to the sounds of words and how to use them. Ray Bradbury said that all writers should read one poem, one essay and one short story every day, and it is a great habit to get into. Especially poetry – how long does it take to read a poem? Start the day by reading a poem – it's much better than reading an email, which is what most of us do.

 Key idea

Read a poem every day to increase your awareness of word choice.

Onomatopoeia

Think of a busy cafeteria: crash, tinkle, crack, bing, ding, ring, clatter, clop, tap. Words that imitate or resemble the sound they describe are called onomatopoeia. They include animal noises like oink and chirrup as well as other words that sound like the sound they make – snap, crackle, pop. I clearly remember the first time I heard the word and thinking it was wonderful. My whole heart just lit up.

If you have a chance at some point when you are just sitting somewhere on one of your listening expeditions, pay attention to the sounds around you and see whether you can find some onomatopoeia, just for the fun of it. As we get serious about writing, we sometimes forget how much joy there is in wordplay. English is a fantastic, wildly expressive language, and you can have a huge amount of fun with it.

 A.A. Patawaran

'Sound gives life to our words just as well as the images they conjure up and the sound is there, whether or not we read them aloud.'

SCENT

Americans are funny about smells. We don't really want anything to *have* a scent. We scour our environments and ourselves to the point that a person smells pretty much the same as a living room and as a freshly laundered sheet.

Even so, at a primal level, we are very much driven by smell, just like dogs and cats and apes. A mother knows the smell of her baby – I could easily tell the difference between my children's clothes, and I'm sure you could, too. Remember the first time you noticed that your boyfriend's coat smelled like him?

Scent is extremely powerful to the mammals we are. In Mandy Aftel's fabulous book about perfume, *Essence and Alchemy,* the author talks about the power of scent to bypass the high-level brain, all the sophisticated parts, and go directly to the primitive limbic system, which is why when you smell your grandmother's perfume you are instantly transported to a day in your childhood. You're not remembering; you're there. I wrote an entire novel centred on this idea – that a person could make perfumes that smell of memories.

Notice scents and smells

Over the next few days, pay attention to scents. Notice how often you use scent to make a decision about something – you smell fruit to see whether it's ripe, your clothes to see whether they're clean, the milk to see whether it's gone off. Notice the smells around you and try not to shy away from them, good and bad.

Pay attention to scents and smells in your fictional world. Layer in the scent of the world of your characters. Think about how to use scent to add to characterization and setting. For example, think of friends who always smell of shampoo. My cat has sweet-smelling fur at all times. Brewing coffee lures us out of bed. Freshly baked bread makes us think of a warm kitchen.

Write about smell

1 Write three sentences filling in these gaps:

'When I smell _____, I remember _____'

2 Now do a five-minute timed writing on one of them.

A memory of scent

Give one of your main characters a memory involving scent.

TASTE

Taste is critical to creating depth in romantic novels. This means not only the taste of a lover's skin or lips, which are very important, of course, but also the taste of food and drink. Eating and drinking are basic drives closely related to the yearning and satisfactions of sex. The feast of love and the feast of life are deeply connected, and there is a great deal of potential in mastering the art of getting taste on to the page.

I am a writer who loves to write about food. When I wrote the following paragraphs in *The Lost Recipe for Happiness*, I knew I'd found this character's voice:

She had to blink to clear her vision after the white-hot sun, and found herself staring at an enormous spread of food in the dun-coloured dining room. Acres of food, in all kinds of colours and textures, their scents mingling in the air like wicked perfume—chocolate and chilli and browning onions and slow-stewed pork. Beneath a black wooden cross covered with tiny silver milagros—tiny hands and eyes and legs and hearts flying across the bottom—the food overflowed Tupperware and glass and thin paper plates stuck together in threes to make them more sturdy.

Elena watched the women swirling around, arranging, putting things out. Most of it was the usual, a cake iced in white and polka-dotted with halved maraschino cherries; a pile of unidentifiable meat, charred and dry; a lumpy stack of flour tortillas; plain white dinner rolls, the kind that came on trays from the supermarket; and chicken, fried and in barbecue sauce.

It was the tomatoes that drew Elena, the sliced red and green and yellow sweet peppers; the fresh sprays of green onion stuck in a glass bowl with their tails sticking out like fans; zucchinis and squashes in sticks; bowls of hot pickled cherry peppers and fresh, gleaming salsas with tiny wheels of green onion bobbing up through the red sea, and a dark green salad dressed with tiny oranges. Things that

*were ripe and fresh in everyone's backyard gardens. Maybe
not the oranges, which she thought came from a can, but
everything else.*

*'Are you hungry, m'ija?' Auntie Gloria was carrying a pile
of tamales to the table. 'You can make a plate if you want.'*

Barbara O'Neil, *The Lost Recipe for Happiness*
(Random House, 2008)

It is not only food that carries flavour. We taste fear and excitement.
We taste a change in the atmosphere when a storm is brewing. We
taste rain and smoke from forest fires.

How can you add more flavour to your work?

Write about taste

1 Sit down with a food item you know well. Taste it in small bites,
taking your time to notice exactly what makes up those tastes.
Make notes.

2 Set a timer for ten minutes and write on the prompt: 'When I
taste _____, I think of _____'

TOUCH

Touch is very important in romantic tales, of course: the feel of hair
swishing, skin touching skin; heat and cold; shivers and reactions.
What do things feel like?

Here is a place to exercise a lot of freshness. Anyone who has ever
read a number of romance novels will be familiar with the first ten
ways you come up with to describe the touch of hands, of lips. Work
hard to put yourself really in the moment and give the reader a fresh
take, which means a great new entry point.

Describing touch

1 What do things feel like? Smooth, rough, scratchy? What else?
Come up with 20 words that describe touch.

2 Go through the novels you've chosen to analyse and read the
way each writer describes moments of touching. What do you
notice? Are there clichés? Can you come up with others? Make a
list for your notebook. Be aware of touch as you continue to read
more books.

Mastering the tools

Here is a list of ten ways you can train yourself to write a richer book every time:

1 Feed your senses.

Take time to do things that feed your senses, all of them. Go to beautiful gardens and museums, fabric stores and restaurants. Smell roses, perfumes and other people.

2 Eavesdrop and stare.

Make a habit of eavesdropping and buy sunglasses so you can stare more easily.

3 Make notes and sketches.

Carry a notebook and make sketches of things. They don't have to be skilled or even competent; they'll just help remind you to really see things. A good second is to make frequent use of your phone camera. If you see something that jolts your senses, take a picture of it.

4 Travel.

Go wherever you can. Go to new neighbourhoods and to faraway places. Pay attention to your surroundings, but also pay attention to how you feel exploring them. Are you excited, standoffish, worried about looking foolish or intruding where you should not go? Notice how things smell the same and different.

5 Listen to music.

Find music you love and play it often. Go to concerts or out to listen to music in whatever venue you can enjoy. Go to plays. Watch movies.

6 Develop hobbies.

Develop hobbies that excite your senses. Visual people might enjoy things like making stained glass or quilts or learning to paint with watercolours. Auditory people might like learning to play an instrument or collecting the music of a certain form or era. (I like the blues and the Baroque.) Texture people might like model-making or sewing. Many writers are magpies, and that's good. If you get a yen to learn to cook Indian food, or learn to speak Arabic, or play the cello, go for it. I promise that, far from taking away from your writing, it will add to it.

7 Read poetry – aloud.

This is something we've moved away from in the West, but writers are the natural audience for poets. Read it and feel it. There is a poet for everyone out there. Find one you love.

8 Flag up your themes.

Be alert to the themes and ideas you love to use in your work. How do you use them? What interests you? How can you keep coming up with fresh ways to illustrate them?

9 Tweak the details.

To make your manuscript really sparkle, spend an extra two weeks working on layering in those colours, on the details of smell and touch and song, and on tweaking a scarf from blue to orange.

10 Enjoy yourself!

Remember to be playful when you are writing: this is about making something beautiful, not a big, impossible challenge.

Gathering telling details

One of the most elevating aspects of writing is the use of detail. It marks voice, it shows attention and care, and it can be quite elegant. However, the main reason for cultivating the powerful use of telling detail in your own work is to transport the reader to another world. Our goal as fiction writers is to remove all barriers to the reader experiencing the story in the purest, truest way possible. Detail is one of the most important ways we do that.

Key idea

Our goal as fiction writers is to remove all barriers to the reader experiencing the story in the purest, truest way possible.

All of the exercises in this chapter will help you store details of many kinds, which will lead to a level of excellence almost by osmosis. You practise good writerly habits like observation and note-taking so that, when you sit down to write, you have a great store of potential elements on which to draw.

To observe those details, resolve to yourself that you will keep your nose out of your smartphone when you are in public. Stay present; look around. If you are a notebook sort, scribble notes. Maybe shoot photos of intriguing details. I take pictures of buildings and windows and thousands of other things, capturing for myself some little something I might use later.

To find those remarkable details, you must open your eyes to your world every day, every moment. Pay attention to what people do, how they gesture, what their eyes do when they are happy and when they are lying and when they are gazing upon the face of someone they love. Pay attention to the details of the way people dress. A baggy pair of khakis worn with a pair of glittery sandals is not the same as a baggy pair of khakis worn with a pair of scuffed boots or white socks and earth sandals or a pair of high heels so battered that the covering has worn away from the heel, showing bits of plastic beneath.

That last detail, the worn high heels with baggy khakis, suggests a lot of story to me. I'm already building a story about this girl. I think she's skinny and young and doesn't have any money.

All fiction is created from detail, of course. Scenes, characters and plots are created out of single molecules of detail that create solid experiences. Unfortunately, a great many stories are crafted from overused, exhausted, bland details, placeholders that do nothing to set the work apart.

Using memorable detail in your work

Not long ago, I participated in a writing retreat in Breckenridge Colorado, where a collection of talented writers showed their work to a panel of people working in the field: writer, agent, editor and poet. We all read the works and met the writers individually. Afterward, Jeff Kleinman, agent at Folio Literary, suggested that we offer some exercises because, in nearly every case, the thing missing from the work of these writers was a sense of depth. Our exercises ended up being nearly entirely about character and focused almost entirely on detail.

I read a lot of material on a regular basis, and I can't say I remember a lot of material from that weekend (with a couple of exceptions), but I clearly and strongly remember a piece Jeff wrote about being happy in Italy, riding a horse at sunset through long grass. It was thick with detail – details of light and the Italian setting and a sense of time. It lingers with me, several months later.

That is the exact thing you want – for the work to be so memorable that it sticks.

 ## Key idea

The purpose of good detail work is to create that sense of compelling recognition in the reader, to anchor and make memorable whatever it is that you are writing about.

How do you do that? An entire book could be written on this subject, of course, and every case is different. In general, the 'telling' part of telling detail means that it is unique, or at least unusual. It's fresh and new. It stands up and captures a moment, a character and a setting in a way that cements it for the reader.

The devil is in the detail

Spend some time this week noticing how writers you admire use detail. Pay attention to the way you are using it in your own work. Are some types of detail easier to manage than others? Is it easier to create settings or characters?

Mostly, you probably need to go deeper: deeper, deeper, deeper. You should know everything there is to know about your characters and your settings. I spend days on character interviews and research before and during the writing of a novel. By the time I get ready to polish a manuscript for the final time, I can walk through a bathroom or bedroom of a character and see exactly what they'd have on the shelves, whether they'd leave clothes on the floor or dishes in the sink. I should know how to shop for them (and have, unfortunately, shopped *as* them) and what their response to almost any question would be. In my settings, I know where things are located, what matters, and try to illuminate those things that will make things live for my reader.

How do you decide which are the compelling details? In my book *The All You Can Dream Buffet,* I tried to convey the enchantment I had felt when I had once seen chickens wandering freely at an organic farm. The thing I kept remembering was the glossiness of the hens' feathers, their lack of fear. I worked it into the manuscript early on, in the setting scene. I had been enchanted by the feathers on those birds, by the friendly way they had clucked along with us, so, I thought, it would probably be something my reader would enjoy as well.

If you can't figure out what details are the most compelling, you can write long lists of them, then discard the obvious and the boring, and work in some that you like best. Another way is to write a lot of detail, then cut back and cut back until you have the spare bones of a Truth. A great Facebook post can do this. Romance writer Eloisa James Facebooked her year in Paris that way, and then published a memoir from the posts.

Increase the power of details

Choose one of the pieces you've written and go back through it to highlight the details that are most compelling. How can you increase the power of those few details and drop the rest?

Here's an example of vivid writing that reflects a particular culture:

> *Cowboy at Tantra Coffeehouse who was telling some gal his mentor is somereincarnated Spanish Conquistador who roamed South Texas, mute for twenty years with a leather pouch. 'He wants ta meetcha,' he told her. Her: 'When?' Him: 'I dunno. Could be tomorrow. Could be a week. He appears when he appears.'*
> Nick Belardes, Facebook post

We know that it's the western United States and that we're dealing with eccentrics here.

Workshop

1 Take a notebook to a place where you can sit and observe people, in their setting. Write down every possible detail about them. Now narrow it down to three details, then to two, then to one. Write the top two details into a sentence of description.

2 Write a character sketch about a relative or family member. In one paragraph, describe the habits that shape this person. What piece of clothing do you see them in? What foods define them?

Example: My grandfather was a charming, hardworking ladies' man. He smoked three packs of Camel non-filters a day until one day in his fifties when he stopped, cold turkey, and never smoked again. It still killed him 20 years later, emphysema weakening him until his heart gave up. What I remember is not the cigarettes or the death, but the curl of black hair that fell on his forehead, and the way he drove his El Camino at breathtaking speed wherever he went, and the mischievous grin that twinkled across his handsome face.

3 Describe the street you live on. Without ever saying what the income level or cultural make-up of the neighbourhood is, show it to me.

Example: Tall trees, generations old, turn red along my street. Cars are discreetly tucked away in their garages or in the driveway.

4 Describe a process you know well: cooking soup, perhaps, or bathing a baby. What single detail can you bring forward to make the process fresh and real for someone? What can you turn upside down to make the reader see the process in a new way? Don't be afraid to be gritty.

Focus point

A great writer knows:

- the entire spectrum of tools and how to use them to create a world that feels absolutely real
- that all five senses matter
- how to use colour
- how to use and manipulate setting and tone
- how to listen to the word choices and sentence rhythms of a piece to help create the effect she wants to create.

Words are the building blocks of everything we do. Use good ones.

Where to next?

In the next chapter, we will dive even more deeply into your personal work by exploring voice, one of the most confusing and important aspects of writing.

11

Finding your unique writing voice

Voice is one of the least understood concepts in all writing, and yet we all know that it is wildly important. As a writing teacher, I travel to conferences to teach workshops, and the most popular of them by far is the one on the writer's voice. This workshop is a deep, hands-on exploration of the elements that create an individual writer's voice: it covers background and culture and the place where you grew up, the books and genres that have shaped your thinking about writing, and the way you perceive and express the world.

In this chapter you will learn to identify the various things that come together to create the individual writer's voice. By doing writing exercises, you will begin to understand what makes your voice unique and how you might be able to apply that to creating more powerful, more authentic work.

What is voice?

We hear editors talk about voice, about buying work because the voice is 'strong'. But what is it, exactly? Some of the questions that seem to come up are:

- What does having a strong voice mean?
- Are some people born with a writing voice and others not?
- What is the difference between style and voice?
- Can you change your voice?

I started teaching workshops on voice because I kept hearing stories of writers who were misdirected, misled and warped by the contest and critique group process (not that there is anything wrong with contests or critique groups). I strongly believe that the work of each writer is valuable and important, and even potentially world changing. Books are mighty things. Writers are the people who create them.

It is my job to tell each of you that who you are as a writer matters. By helping you uncover your voice, I enable you to be freer to write the stories only you can tell.

 Key idea

If you don't write your books, they might not ever get written.

Voice is the most powerful tool you have in your entire toolbox. It's part of you, as distinct as a fingerprint, and not erasable. So you don't have the choice of using it or not using it – it's part of everything you do. Just as you start to know who is talking on an email loop, just as you know exactly to whom you're speaking when your mother calls you, you are identifiable, too.

What does happen is that voices get watered down, corrupted, twisted, by all sorts of processes. One of them is the critique group process, which can be valuable but also destructive to individual voices. Another is the contest process, where mechanics are often valued over the raw beauty of an emerging voice. Some corruptions come from within, as internalized voices from childhood that say who we are is not quite right, and therefore must be changed. There are many others, and you may stumble over some of your corrupting influences in these exercises. Sometimes this can be an emotional process, but that's OK.

The great pleasure in excavating and nourishing your own particular, unique voice is that, once you do it, you are suddenly a much stronger writer. You're telling your own stories. You're more confident in your choices, and you're more able to match your particular voice to the market for a much better chance of success.

Note: this is a very heavily exercise-based chapter. The timed exercises will be illuminating if you do them on your own, but even more so if you find a partner to do them with you, or even a small group of writers.

Your family and culture

Once I would have heard the old adage 'Write what you know', and thought, ugh! What could I possibly offer the writing world? The most exciting thing about my cultural background was that my father ate baloney sandwiches with mustard.

Of course, I eventually realized that that was not really true. While there are cultures and geographical areas that seem to be particularly well represented in writing, we all come from a particular place and time, just as our characters do. As a writer, I had to recognize and claim my life before I could get to the truth of my work.

And what happened was that when I finally wrote a romance novel set in the town where I lived, grappling with the real things going on around me, it was infused with my voice and it sold. That first book was about blue-collar people with artistic leanings, living in a city with Vietnam vets and a steel mill collapsing and many ethnic influences.

Voice is not something you can avoid using, but sometimes we want to try to cover up our origins. All that does is lead to something that doesn't sound authentic. One of my students said this: 'Sometimes, when you meet an author that you have read, you realize how much they sound like their books. Maybe it is their choice of words and syntax and how they pour themselves into a story, bringing everything with them.'

This is evident to me so often. My friend Christie Ridgway's books sound just like the way she talks. I can hear her clearly in her books. I'm sure that you have had this experience if you have worked with writers in a group setting.

Speaking voice to writing voice helps clarify the point that you have certain elements of your voice that you can't change. Some portions of it might, but it will always be your voice, no one else's. Biologically, it has a certain timbre and tone, and your ethnic and cultural influences, your local region and the languages spoken around you add particularities that make your voice your own.

Write about yourself

These exercises are all timed writings. Set a timer and keep your hand moving, writing for three minutes on each of these prompts.

'The house I lived in when I was seven years old…'

'I am 12 years old…'

'I am 18 years old…'

What do you see if you put these all together? Is there a pattern of revelation? Is there a setting or a geography of your own life? Remember the quote from Rudolph Hinojosa-Smith: 'Place is the spine of a writer.' This is your spine.

There are reasons I chose these particular ages:

- **At seven years old** we are just becoming aware of ourselves as a being separate from our parents, families and teachers. You are suddenly a person. You. Seven-year-olds are often idealistic, too. They want to see the world as a good place, a supportive place, and will come up with great ideas for healing or helping. Ideas that take root at this age often stay with us for the rest of our lives. When I was seven the United States was very polluted and the ecological movement was taking hold in a powerful way. I kept trying to motivate the students and adults in my world to pick up litter. Interestingly, my town is very clean these days, and I am still devoted to ecological ideas. Can you see a link like that in your own life?

Your characters at age seven

Where did each of your main characters live at age seven?

- **At 12 years old** we enter the non-adult, non-child world of adolescence. Often, big changes are going on in our bodies and we feel like aliens and it's all about trying to fit in.
- **At 18 years old** we are technically adults, heading out into the world. More writers have shared absolutely crushing stories about being 18 than any other age. We often make decisions that can't be rectified or undone at age 18 and then live with the consequences for the rest of our lives. These may include getting married too young, not going to college, going to the wrong college, listening too much to others and not taking good advice. It's pretty big stuff to have to do when you don't have much experience.

Your characters at 18

Did either of your characters make a big mistake at 18?

Write about your family and culture

Sometimes we feel contempt for what is familiar. When you were a child, what embarrassed you? Write for three minutes on the first two prompts:

'My culture is…'

'What embarrassed me about my family/culture/neighbourhood was…'

Write for four minutes on: 'A food from my childhood was…'

These are pretty self-explanatory. They reveal the powerful culture that you call your own. And they are all potent in one way or another. Did anything surprise you? Did anything sting?

Understand that you do not *have to* write about your own landscape, but seeing what it is will ground you in your voice in a way nothing else can. Those cadences, those foods, the way people talked to you, all of this is very influential on your speaking voice and, as pointed out above, the speaking voice and writing voice are often quite closely connected.

Speaking and writing voice

I am a Colorado native, born to Texas 'transplants' who talked to me in their east Texas accent while I was learning to speak, so I had a bit of a drawl until I went to school. This shows up now and then, especially if I'm disciplining children.

I also grew up in neighbourhoods where there were many Hispanic families, so that Spanish syllabic softening creeps into my words and word choices. I also lived in Pueblo, Colorado, for 20 years, and the city has a particular accent that's pervasive and difficult to resist. It keys into both the rural West and the Hispanic layering and gives a singsong quality to speech. (I wrote about this accent in *No Place Like Home*, set in Pueblo, and I swear to you I could pick it out anywhere in the world.)

Of course, I am also a university-educated writer and I have learned to speak clearly and concisely. Some portions of my voice will change according to the audience or group I'm speaking with. If I'm hanging out in Pueblo with a bunch of friends, I'll fall pretty naturally into the local lilt. When I go north to be with friends who are all from other countries (South Africa, Germany, UK, etc.), I discover that the lilt diminishes, but it's still there.

If I am speaking to a group or having a business dinner or discussion, I have a nearly 'accentless' American delivery, though I notice that it's nearly impossible to get rid of the very Western rise at the end of my sentences.

I also have slight lisp. It's always there. I also have a particular cadence to my voice, which is a little breathless and fast, and a timbre that is the biology of my voice box. Those things don't change. They are my voice.

What influences your voice?

Can you trace some of the influences on your speaking voice? Your writing voice is as much your own as your speaking voice, and they are often influenced by the same things.

More exercises in voice

The outcome of the following exercise may surprise you and lead you in unexpected directions. It may lead you to discover aspects of your voice that you had not thought of before.

Write out more lists

Return to your list of 25 favourite things that you compiled for the exercise in Chapter 10. Remember that you picked out your primary sense.

Now you can discover more about your voice by listing some favourite things in more detail. Don't overthink this exercise; just write down things as they occur to you.

1 What are your top ten favourite movies?

2 What was your favourite book at the age of around 15?

3 What is the favourite book you have read in the past six months?

This exercise takes many of my students by surprise – and often reveals something to them that they have not understood about their tastes. One writer had been pursuing category romance for several years, thinking that it would be a good place for her to break into the genre (and it sometimes can be). She was not having much luck. When she examined what this exercise revealed to her, it was plain that her tastes sometimes ran rather strongly toward the paranormal, and so she wrote an urban fantasy series that sold. Another student came up with a dark Young Adult idea that was completely different from the other things she'd been doing.

Question your assumptions

What have you believed about your writing that might not be true?

VOICE VERSUS STYLE

One of the ideas that gets mixed up is voice versus style. Voice is your body; style are the clothes you put on it. One is fixed; the other can be changed.

Key idea

Voice is a potato; style is a French fry.

You might write horror or erotica or mysteries and skip between them daily, but your essential voice – your body – will stay the same. Your style will slide into the uniform required by the genre.

To get a feeling for what that looks like, try these exercises.

Write in three subgenres

1 Write three paragraphs about a character in a romance novel: hero or heroine, it doesn't matter which.

2 Now write three paragraphs about that same character, but now he or she is starring in a horror novel.

3 Now write three paragraphs for the same character again, but this time he or she is starring in a mainstream literary novel.

Workshop

This exercise will help you identify all the elements that go to make up your unique voice.

1 Where did you grow up? What languages and accents predominate in that area?

2 Who taught you to talk? Do your parents have an accent of any kind? Did anyone ever speak a language other than English around you / to you?

3 What were the main ethnic groups around you when you grew up?

   If there's a predominant ethnic group in that geography, do you know any of the stories/legends/superstitions of that group? Did any of them stick with you particularly when you were a child?

4 Have you ever felt a particular affinity for a geography or culture that is not your own? If so, why? What about it do you love or identify with?

5 What did you love more than anything on earth when you were 12 years old? What did you want to be then?

6 What are your top five favourite novels of all time? What was your favourite book when you were 12 and when you were 14?

7 Which writer and which book inspired you to want to be a writer?

8 What book do you most wish you'd written? Why? What parts of it make you swoon? Characters? Voice? Plot? (Try typing a few pages from it, just to see how it feels to you. Where would you change the flow of the language, the way the paragraphs are broken?)

9 What are your obvious passions and hobbies?

10 What are the defining characteristics of these passions? (For example, gardeners and photographers are usually interested in light and colour. Model builders and cross-stitchers tend to like attention to detail.)

11 What would five friends all say about you if someone asked them to name your defining passion?

12 What are your secret passions?

13 What charities speak to you? What one world or national ill would you fix magically if you could? What world sorrows can move you to tears?

14 If you weren't a writer but could be any other kind of artist/musician, what would you choose? What would be your tools? Why?

15 Now focus on your own work:
   – Do you notice yourself returning to certain themes?
   – Are there times/places that you use repeatedly? If so, can you identify the reasons they appeal to you, and if so, are there other times/places that might also stimulate your passions? Have you ever tried to use those other places/times?
   – What do readers/editors/outsiders seem to respond to most enthusiastically in your work? Is there anything that they see as a strength that you don't notice or value?
   – What would you *like* people to say about your voice?
   – If you could only write one book in your life, what book would it be? Why aren't you writing it?

Now, if you can, try to condense all these defining things into a paragraph or, even better, one sentence: 'My voice is…'

As an example, my paragraph would be:

> People respond to the emotionally intense themes in my work, and to the lyrical or poetic angles in the way I put words down. [Don't be modest! This is for you. No one else ever has to see it.] *I write about cross-cultural themes, food, animals, and I'm drawn to a sheen of magical realism. Colour, light, textures, sounds – everything sensual – matter a lot to me.*

My sentence might be distilled to:

> *My voice is lyrical, emotionally intense and magical.*

What is your voice like?

Focus point

Voice is the culmination of everything in your life: where you grew up, who taught you to talk, your education and cultural background, every friend and enemy you've ever had, everything you've ever smelled or tasted or touched or loved (details, remember?). It's everything: the sum of you.

Where to next?

In the next chapter, we'll talk about how to actually get your writing done.

12

From rough draft to polished draft

How will you become one of the people who actually writes a book instead of one who only wishes she had? We know that around 84 per cent of the population sometimes thinks about getting a book written. It is a pervasive and much-loved idea.

In this chapter we'll examine the physical and psychological tricks that can help you actually get the words on the page and also find your most productive times and locations for writing. We'll look at how to overcome the common excuses for not writing, with strategies such as the '20-minute window' and the 'early-morning window', and how to discover your own natural patterns for maximizing productivity.

Nora Roberts

'You can fix anything but a blank page.'

What are your excuses?

First let's grapple with excuses. Everyone has them and, believe me, I've heard them all: demanding jobs, demanding families, demanding jobs *and* families. Volunteer duties. Not a morning person, not a night person, not a weekend person.

What are some of your excuses? Let's get to the bottom of them.

Write about your excuses

Take out your notebook and set a timer for seven minutes. When you are ready, use the prompt below to start writing, and keep going for the full seven minutes. If you can't think of anything new, just keep writing the same things over and over again. Remember: keep your hand moving. The reason a timed writing works is because it blasts past the editor in you and, with this exercise, you really have to find ways to trick her.

'The things standing between my writing and me are…'

What did you write down? My own excuses are different from day to day, but I have a few that reign supreme: the noise of the world and the Internet, which is just a really big slice of world living on my desk all the time. How seductive to click my mouse and step into that world!

One of the biggest excuses is always 'lack of time'. It may be true that you do not have the time to write all day, but if you really want to write a book, you'll work out where you do have some time to give. Otherwise your books will not get written. And a single book can change the world for ever, or at least give someone some relief from life for a few hours.

Writing requires good habits. I've assembled my basic practices here. You will do doubt find more tricks and tips as you move along the writing process.

Writing the rough draft

There is an idea in the world that writing is a very difficult business, that 'all you have to do is open a vein' and bleed all over the page, or suffer for every word.

This is hogwash. Every year, thousands and thousands of writers commit to NaNoWriMo, National Novel Writing Month, which requires them to write 50,000 words in 30 days. A lot of people manage it, too, and over 100 of those books have gone on to be published by such renowned publishing houses as Random House, Plume, Penguin, HarperCollins and others. The point is not to get a finished book done but to get a rough draft done in that time.

If you want to write a book, you probably already have everything you need to do it – an idea, a sense of how a book flows and some skill with words. To write, what you have to do is sit down and actually do it. Find the best times to work and then make a commitment to yourself and the book you are writing to show up and get it done, day after day after day, week after week, month after month. To write 50,000 words in 30 days, one has to write 1,666 words per day. How long does it take you to write your rough draft?

Anne Lamott

'Perfectionism is the voice of the oppressor, the enemy of the people. It will keep you cramped and insane your whole life, and it is the main obstacle between you and a shitty first draft.'

The rough draft is not meant to be a work of art on any level. It's meant to be you telling yourself a story, plain and simple, so you can see what you have in mind. It can be awkward and stilted. It can backtrack and be littered with lots of notes and marks to remind you to check something. It doesn't have to have the perfect research in place: do you really need to know exactly what sort of lamp would be in this room right now, or (more likely) could you get by with a 'TK' (meaning that more material is 'to come' in journalese) and fill it in later?

The reason that writing is hard is all about the voice in your head that tells you that you're doing it wrong, that you are stupid for trying. It's the mean voice of that teacher you had rolling his eyes over your earnest attempt to do something beautiful. We all have them. Tell them to go away and allow you the pleasure of continuing to tell yourself this story.

Elizabeth Gilbert, the author of the hugely successful memoir *Eat, Pray, Love*, has a wonderful TED talk on giving over some of the responsibility of writing to the daemons who were once thought to have inspired all writing and painting and other art. It's their job to work with you on these projects, so you don't have to take all the responsibility for doing it yourself. Your only job is to turn up and be ready, to put your hands on the keyboard and start writing whatever the daemons tell you to write.

 Key idea

How do you write a rough draft? You show up, over and over, until you reach the end. It is that simple and that hard.

Managing time and finding your rhythms

Sure, you say, just show up. But what if you have a full-time job or kids, or both? What if there seems to be no time to write?
There always is. Thousands of us (including me) have written entire books while juggling children, jobs, spouses, teaching and so forth. What you have to do under these circumstances is discover what works for you. Below are a couple of ideas.

THE 20-MINUTE WINDOW

The late great Ray Bradbury, who is one of my writing heroes in case you hadn't noticed, often said that a writer should begin writing before he lets the world in. That means before television, before conversations, before anything else happens.

In my world – and maybe yours, too – this has not often been a realistic possibility. I've rarely lived alone since I married, and children and partners are people I want to enjoy being with over breakfast. Anyway, it's not realistic to jump out of bed and run to the computer or the notebook. After breakfast, I like to tidy things up and the dog then wants a walk, by which time my head is filled with a lot of non-writing things, like bills and juggling my ever-shrinking hours, which do seem to have gone from 60 minutes to about 40, and when I might be able to get out to get some new jeans, because winter is coming.

All those busy, monkey-mind thoughts are not helpful for creating the ease that is best for writing. All that chatter makes it hard to sort through the billion sentences in my head, the news from the television this morning, the email from a friend…

So I have created a 20-minute window that belongs to me, to my writing right after breakfast. I do not clean up the kitchen. I do not fold the blankets left out on the sofa from the night before, or collect the books I've flung hither and yon (I seem to always be in the middle of three or four). I ignore the pleading eyes of the Saddest Dog in the World and take my freshly filled coffee cup upstairs. I set the timer for 20 minutes, and write whatever comes up. Sometimes it's a blog. Sometimes it's a scene that will come later in the book, and I write fast, without a lot of correction, to get the flavour of the thing down on the page.

I sometimes even just write a journal. Sometimes, a juicy way to get things moving is to write what the Law of Attraction folks call a Rampage of Appreciation, which is to write down all the things you are grateful for in your life, like your child's amazing eyes and warm socks and the little goddess statue on the desk. It almost doesn't matter what it is. It's 20 minutes of writing about whatever I want.

There are two major things this exercise accomplishes. First, I warm up the writing muscles. It shuts the door to the monkey mind and all the noisy voices wanting attention and walks me down the corridor of my mind to the Writing Work Room, which is where all my writing stuff is. Once the door is open for the day, I find it much easier to move in and out, take breaks, head back down the corridor to go back to work, as often as I like. Once I'm actually in the Writing Work Room in my head, with its lovely views and rows and rows of books and articles and novellas and hundreds of other things I've written, I remember that this really is one of my favourite places. All my favourite things are here, all the most authentic things about my life and work.

The second thing it does is remind me how little time it actually takes to put words on the page if I am actually showing up to do it. I've been writing this section for 14 minutes and I have 626 words on the page. In an hour, that's 2,500 words, which is a great writing day by almost anyone's standards.

Now, I know that I won't produce 2,500 words in an hour, hour after hour. It just doesn't work that way. Over the course of an hour, I pause, go back to rewrite and fiddle with things and scowl over word choices, all the things we all do. I try an action paired with a line of dialogue, realize it isn't right, and try something else.

But I do know, because I do it so often, that I can write 600 words pretty reliably in 20 minutes. How many 20-minute segments are there in a day? How many times have you sat in a waiting room, in the car park queue or in the work cafeteria for 20 minutes after lunch?

Even that single 20-minute segment, as early in the day as it can be managed, can be a big win for a busy person seeking time to write. Yes, it's lovely to have oceans of time and submerge yourself in them and the book, but what if you don't have them?

The final winning aspect of the 20-minute window is the fact that it often ends up being much more. If I just open that door, sometimes I don't come out again for hours. That's a really big win.

Have you ever tried the 20-minute window? Can you spy a window early in your day when you might be able to try this? Are there other windows in your day that you might never have noticed?

(There: 21 minutes, 930 words.)

Write for 20 minutes

Set your timer for 20 minutes and write anything you like. Write about your dog or your view or a fight you had with your sister, or anything else. Write anything, but just keep doing it for 20 minutes.

Now count your words. Surprised?

THE EARLY-MORNING WINDOW

Akin to the 20-minute window is the early-morning window. During a particularly crushing deadline period, I forced myself to get up early every day and get my writing done. And remarkably, I discovered that I could write more in the 90 minutes between 4:30 and 6:00 a.m. than at any other time of day.

This is likely to be part of the 'writing before the world comes in', the Bradbury injunction, but I don't care what it is. It works for me, so much so that I've shifted my life around quite a bit in order to accommodate my desire to get at the computer by 4:30. It isn't always easy, but I can do 2,500 to 3,000 words in that time if I'm very motivated. That's worth getting up for.

Maybe you are not a lark like me, but an owl who likes to write at night. It doesn't actually matter what time it turns out to be, but if you can find those magic hours, you will be astonished at the co-operation your brain gives you.

Can you find an hour early in the morning or late at night to get some extra writing time in?

Get around your excuses

OBSERVING YOUR PROCESS

How can you find your own best writing routines? Don't make assumptions about anything to do with your writing. Instead, use the scientific method to study and make observations about your process. Try things, record your observations and draw conclusions.

I highly recommend the booklet *2K to 10K*, written by Rachel Aaron, who had an infant to look after and book contracts to fulfil. She made a chart to study her own work habits and it has been an immensely valuable study for me, too. Check it out at: http://thisblogisaploy.blogspot.com/2011/06/how-i-went-from-writing-2000-words-day.html.

Even though I had been writing for more than 20 years at the time I found her blog post, I was trying to return to a level of productivity that I'd let slip for quite a while. There were new projects knocking on my door and I wanted to find some time to explore them, so I decided to give it a try.

The system is a simple one. It uses a worksheet with grids for filling out the date, the project, a time log (start and finish), number of words, and number of words per hour, and a section for notes (Did I get a lot of sleep? Listen to music? Write away from home?). I committed to observing my processes for a few months, then draw conclusions.

It was shocking to me how little time it actually took to get my words done each day (often as little as two hours) unless I was feeling stressed, when it took longer because I was allowing other things to get in the way of work rather than the work itself. I thought it was impossible for me to write in the afternoons, but it turns out that my second most productive time each day is 12:30–2:30 p.m. Because I thought it was unproductive time, I had scheduled my workouts during that time. When I realized that late morning was actually when I flagged creatively, I could juggle that around without guilt (bonus: the pool and gym are often deserted at that time of day). I highly recommend studying your own habits, too.

Keep a log

Keep a log of your writing time for a few months to see what works best for you.

The important thing, the only thing, is to make a priority of your writing. That's the only way it ever gets done. The other things will help you find your best times, teach you when you are most productive and alert, but only you can make the commitment to actually do it. Write until you've finished a book.

Key idea

Only you can make the commitment to finish a book.

Ernest Hemingway

'The first draft of everything is shit.'

Workshop

By now you have assembled characters, plot, emotional arc and synopis. You are armed with knowledge about your own best creative times, and you understand your excuses. It's time to write the book.

Begin, and write as close to every day as you can manage until you have a whole rough draft. When you finish, give yourself a juicy reward.

If you like, you can email me, too, at barbara@barbaraoneal. com. In the subject line, write: 'I finished my novel!' And in the body, tell me how long it is, what genre, and how many pages. I won't read or critique your novel for you, or recommend where to publish it or anything like that, but I can definitely cheer your accomplishment.

Revising

Once you have finished your first draft, then what? First of all, set it aside for a time. The longer you can let it cool, the better (within reason). This is the time to seek out sympathetic readers. By that I mean people who will be thoughtful and smart about feedback, not stupid and cruel. People who love the kind of book you've written are best, and if they have any writing skill or experience, so much the better. This is a good time to use your critique group, if you have a good one. Solicit their comments.

It's important to remember that everybody's rough drafts are just that – rough. It's meant to be merely a sketch of what the final book is going to look like. It's in later drafts that you get to erase and rearrange your novel and make it gorgeous.

Workshop

Follow these steps when revising your first draft:

1 Sit down with your draft and read through it. When you read something you like, put a star in the margin. When you don't like something, just make a simple checkmark. I use 'DIB', which means Do It Better. The point is not to judge the manuscript, but to get ready to edit it.

2 Make a note of the themes that are showing up and the images your subconscious has coughed up. Trust me: you'll have both of these things. They might be a little soft at this point, but try to find some images you can work with. You might see motifs of water or repeat images of birds or... whatever. Just notice anything that seems to resonate.

3 Once you've done your read-through, go directly to the computer and make your own notes on what is working and what is not working, just as if you were an editor. At this point add the notes and comments of your readers, if you have them.

4 Make an action list of things that need to be done. If a character is failing, your job is to work out why and come up with ways to fix that. If the setting is thin, or the

sexual tension is too soft, make notes. Give your list two parts: things that need fixing, and how the repairs will be done. This isn't easy, but having an action plan will take some of the sting and struggle out of the process and make it much more manageable.

5 Polish to a shine. Once you've done your repairs, go through each scene one at a time to layer in the things the book needs. If it feels slow or soft or dull, try out some things to see what might make it better. Again, go back to your primary senses. What are the colours in this book? What is the setting and how are you putting that on the page – are you using all five senses? Where can you add imagery to underline your theme? (For example, in a book about ghosts, I used images of the Day of the Dead – marigolds and skeletons).

6 Do one more read-through, but this time read the book aloud. This will reveal more flaws than almost any other technique. You'll hear clunky language, catch repetitive works, or notice that you have used the word 'luminous' 16 times. It'll help you catch plodding language and places where you've just missed making a paragraph sing.

7 Finally, make one more pass, polishing, removing repetitive words (there will always be a couple of words that are overused in any manuscript), smoothing it all out one more time. Check characterization, plot, emotional arc, subplots and ending.

Focus points

1 Write whole books. Don't write bits and pieces here and there, writing half of a scene on this one, and a chapter or two over here. Choose a book, make a commitment and finish that book before you move on to another one.

2 Write the first draft without judging. Let it arrive and be itself; let it show itself to you. By the time you've reached the end on the first pass, many of the book's themes and colours and ideas will all be much easier to see.

3 Try to resist showing the rough draft to anyone until it is finished. Everyone means to be helpful, but the only vision that matters in this book is yours. Let it emerge. Write the story your way, and *then* let people in.

4 Write regularly. Every day is the optimum, but get as many writing days into every week as possible. Some writers make a commitment to 100 words per day, which might not seem like much, but it adds up to a couple of pages a week, every week. What it really does is help you create healthy writing habits.

Where to next?

In the next chapter you'll find out what publishing options are available for the romantic fiction writer and how to decide which one to choose.

13

Publishing

Once you've finished and polished a book, what's the next step? How do you go about finding the right path for your book, especially now that there are so many different ways to publish?

In this chapter you will learn what kinds of publishing options are available for today's romantic fiction writer. We will discuss the pros and cons of traditional publishing, indie publishing, small publishers and digital-only publishing and how to make good decisions about them.

Nicholas Sparks

'Publishing is a business. Writing may be art, but publishing, when all is said and done, comes down to dollars.'

Studying the market

The three ways to publish in the current market are:

- through a traditional publisher who pays an advance and offers royalties
- via indie or self-publishing
- through a small press.

The lines between these various modes have blurred quite a lot in recent years (for example, many traditional publishers who once paid advances now have digital-only lines that do not pay advances), but these are the three main directions a romantic novelist has to go. How do you know which is the best way for you?

By the time you've finished writing your book, you will have read many, many romantic novels and you should have some idea of who publishes the kind of book you've written. Romantic women's fiction is published by many different houses and many editors enjoy reading it, for example; while if you wish to write a traditional sheik romance, you'll probably be writing for Harlequin. Do your research to find out who publishes the books you write. (*The Writers' & Artists' Yearbook* in the UK and the *Writer's Market* in the United States are the classic places to start.)

Because the options have changed so much in recent years, let's break down the pros and cons in each of the main choices: traditional publishing, small press publishing and indie publishing. I have experience with all three and a pretty clear understanding of them.

What are your goals?

What are your publishing goals? What do you hope to accomplish with your writing? Do you want to appeal to millions or just get a book out there? Is money or fame a major motivator, or do you need respect? If you had to narrow it down to the one person you couldn't wait to tell you had a book out, who would it be and what would his response be?

TRADITIONAL PUBLISHING

In traditional publishing, the model still mostly follows a familiar pattern. A writer writes a novel, finds an agent, and the book is offered to editors who work for major publishing houses with the money to pay advances and royalties. The author is offered a contract, which the agent negotiates, and then an editor helps the author shape the book into the best possible form for publication. In this model, the publisher shoulders all the costs of design, cover, printing and distribution in return for a large percentage of the profits, usually between 85 and 93 per cent. The author share tends to be around 10 per cent, of which the agent will collect 15 per cent.

If the only lens you are using is money, this sounds like a very bad bargain. However, publishing houses offer hundreds of years of experience. Editors tend to be well educated, experienced in the genre they work in and passionate about the books they buy. (To be an editor can be prestigious, but it is not a particularly well-paid position until you rise in the ranks. I've known many a young New York editor who lived in a studio apartment with two others in a fifth-floor walkup in Brooklyn.) There is an art department staffed with talented people, and book designers who have experience with making books look fantastic.

The book will undergo content editing, line editing, and then copy-editing, all of which helps ensure that the book will go out into the world clean and without errors that will embarrass you later (though not always: I wrote a historical romance set in the eighteenth century in which the characters reference *The Three Musketeers*, a book that had not yet been written. Believe me, readers let me know).

It will then go out to reviewers and the sales force will take it to their accounts and all the work of getting the books into the outlets where it will sell is done for you. Your job is only to let the world know it has arrived, appear at any events the publisher has arranged for you (probably not many in the current market) and hope you sell a lot of books.

Key idea

It must be said that traditional publishing offers the most prestige. Without the bulk of a major traditional publisher behind your book, it's virtually impossible to be reviewed in any major newspapers, be considered for literary awards or find any other literary anointing. Have you dreamed of being traditionally published by a particular house or imprint?

A major benefit of traditional publishing is payment through advances and royalties. Advances have been falling in recent years as computers make it a lot easier to make true calculations of what a book might earn, but they can still be a great way to get paid. They can be a headache, too, because they come in sporadically and sometimes unpredictably, but getting a solid chunk of cash makes things possible in life that are not always possible with the usual salary. This can lead to what my beloved calls 'advance addiction', which is a condition where sufferers will do anything to get that next advance, even to the detriment of their long-term interests.

The downside to the model is that, while you don't have to do any of the work of actual publishing, you also have no control. You will not have much input on cover design, pricing, release dates or anything else. You control the writing, and that's it. Traditional publishing also moves very slowly. From the time you turn a book in to the day it is published, it's usually about a year, sometimes longer.

You will also almost certainly need an agent, which can be a very good thing or a very bad thing, depending on which one you choose. Agents serve as publishers' gatekeepers and it can be difficult to land a high-ranking one. (There is more on agents below.)

SELF-PUBLISHING AND INDIE PUBLISHING

 Lori Lesko

'The good news about self-publishing is you get to do everything yourself. The bad news about self-publishing is you get to do everything yourself.'

Until about five years ago, only losers or determined visionaries ever seriously self-published. Then, with the advent of digital publishing and the e-reader, the opportunities for writers to self-publish surged.

I was on the sidelines when the first writers began to break out. I met one of those writers, Barbara Freethy, at an RWA conference in San Francisco early in my career. I might have had two books out with Silhouette, but no more than that. I happened to sit with this other young mother at a luncheon and we talked about the thrill of publishing our first books, and about children, and all those things.

Over the years, we ran into each other now and then, experiencing many of the ups and downs that commercial fiction writers experience. She started writing women's fiction a little before I did, and landed a prestigious agent. I changed directions a couple of times, also went through a couple of agents, and finally found a place writing romantic women's fiction with a single editor who 'got' me.

As time went by, Barbara and I had more in common, more friends, more experiences. One of my best friends was a good friend of hers and we spent more time together, talking about the ups and down (and ups and downs and ups and downs). A group of us talked via email regularly and had drinks at conferences.

In 2010 the economy was wrecked and the digital wars were beginning. Amazon rose to power, the US bookstore chain Borders crashed and print runs plummeted for most of us. Barbara had two children in college, a husband who was a contractor in a market that had just been destroyed, and a sinking feeling that she might not get another contract from her publisher. She had to do something.

She poured herself into learning about the indie market, studying covers and presentations and back-cover copy. She taught herself to make great covers in PhotoShop, figured out how to format and upload her books into the available venues, and doggedly published a considerable number of her backlist titles.

Things began to take off: the numbers were going up and up, so fast that she and her husband couldn't stop checking. Take a walk; check the numbers. Eat dinner; check the numbers. They were giddy with disbelief – and delight. Within three years, she was making seven figures a year and had sold over 4 million books. She is the bestselling Amazon author of all time.

Life changing! Barbara is now one of the most cited, most highly respected of the indie-publishing success stories. There are many of them. Some depend on luck and timing, but most require a lot of blood, sweat and tears.

The pros of indie publishing are simple: money, speed and control. Because the writer either does the work or contracts to have it done for her, she keeps a much larger portion of the profits (70 per cent on average). If a book takes off, that can be a lot of money, money that puts advances to shame. I personally know more than five writers who have made millions in self-publishing. Some were previously published, some were not, but all have continued to earn six or seven figures several years in a row now.

There is also the speed factor. With indie publishing, it's possible to change covers in a day, publish a series once a week or once a month, change direction any time you feel the need. A book can be finished, then edited and published in a matter of weeks rather than a year. This applies to all aspects of traditional versus indie publishing: everything about traditional publishing moves slowly because the machine is so vast. Everything about indie publishing is fleet and sharp. (This can have downsides. Many, many books have been published before they should have been.)

Which books are self-published?

Browse the top 100 lists in romance, women's fiction or historical romance on Amazon or one of the other major digital sales outlets online. Can you tell which books are self-published?

Finally, control is all in the hands of the writer. This is one of the most appealing aspects of self-publishing for many of us, including me. I have an extensive backlist to which I'd procured the rights and, with the help of an assistant, managed to publish it all. The ability to keep changing a cover until one clicked was huge, and when I want to put something on sale – say for a holiday or to promote a connected book – I can do that.

The challenges with indie publishing lie mainly in the enormous workload and the need either to learn how to format and understand good cover art and book design, or to hire someone to do these tasks. You must also hire editors, copy-editors and proofreaders, services that are not inexpensive. You are no longer just the author but also the product manager. You need a great amount of knowledge and the risks of getting it wrong are high.

Key idea

If you choose to go down the indie route, do your homework. Network with other authors, pay attention to who is doing good cover work and what looks terrible, and be willing to fail before you succeed.

What's your opinion?

Do you read indie-published work? Do you feel the public respects it less or more than traditionally published fiction?

HYBRID AND SMALL PUBLISHERS

Lying between the so-called Big Five (or is it four now?) publishers and indie publishers are the digital-only traditional publishers and small publishers.

Digital-only publishing has been around for a while, but has grown in popularity over the past few years, with nearly all the major romantic fiction and women's fiction publishers offering a line that goes straight to digital. Examples are Flirt (New Adult) and Loveswept imprints from Random House, Carina Press from Harlequin and Impulse from Avon.

This can be a very appealing option for some writers: since much romance has been published in mass-market paperback and the outlets for that work have been shrinking to practically nothing, it makes sense. More and more readers no longer shop for physical books but browse online for their books in digital format and fill their e-readers in the same way they once filled their shopping bags.

The terms for digital-only deals can take two forms. Some imprints offer the choice between traditional advance/royalty structures or a no-advance 50/50 split of profits. The publisher does the usual work of editing, proofing, cover and book design and distribution, and there is a bit more cachet in being published by a major house.

Look at digital imprints

Go online and see how many digital imprints you can find, and what kind of terms they each offer.

SMALL PRESS

There are small digital presses and small traditional presses. Some are very successful and some are not. They offer what each of the others offers, but usually on a smaller scale. Do your research and be absolutely sure you are with a viable, royalty-paying publisher before you sign on.

Thomas Wolfe

'Publishing is a very mysterious business. It is hard to predict what kind of sale or reception a book will have, and advertising seems to do very little good.'

Agents

To be able to submit to a traditional publisher, you will need an agent. They provide gatekeeping and an introduction to publishers that a writer on her own would have trouble matching.

 Jacqueline Carey

'Having a literary agent makes a huge difference in submitting work. My agent has access and tremendous passion.'

There is no licensing process for agents. Anyone with a yen can hang out a sign and start representing authors, so never pay an agent anything until he has sold something for you. It is acceptable to pay some fees, such as messengers and carriage, and subsidiary rights agents will take 20 per cent, but, in general, an agent should take only 15 per cent and then only when she has sold something.

All the warnings aside, a good agent can be worth all the treasures of Arabia. Look for someone who, first of all, loves your work, then someone who has plenty of connections in your world. Read the acknowledgements and dedication pages in your favourite novels, and join Publishers Lunch (http://lunch.publishersmarketplace.com/) for searchable databases of who has made sales to which editors.

 Key idea

The most important thing to remember about agents is that it is better to have no agent than to have a bad one.

Conferences

Many writing conferences are held every year. They are a great place in which to meet other writers, and they may also give you a chance to pitch your work to editors and agents and meet people in the business in a way that can be sociable and enjoyable. It can help you get your book read, get it in front of the right people, and lead to better and better things.

But keep it in perspective. Your whole life and career do not hang in the balance at a single conference. Make the most of the opportunities, but remember that there will be others if this one doesn't work out.

Branding, social media and marketing

The subject of what happens after you publish your book is so vast that it needs a book of its own, and there are many out there. The main point to take away from this book is that your job will not end when you publish. You will be asked by your publisher to participate, sometimes in very time-consuming ways, in the marketing of that book. You will be expected to have, at a minimum, a Facebook account, a Twitter account and a webpage. You will probably need to blog for other people and yourself. A writer in today's world is a public person. Learn how to manage the flow of information through you and about you by studying those who offer the illusion of intimacy without actually giving away too much.

Focus point

Here is a table of the pros and cons of the two main routes to publication, for comparison.

	Traditional publishing	Indie publishing
Pros	Prestige	Potential earnings
	Advances	Control
	Editorial, packaging and sales support	Speed
Cons	Very small share of the profits	Workload
	Lack of control	The need to know all the elements of actual publishing
	Slow publishing times	Start-up costs

Where to next?

In the next and final chapter, I'll give you a pep talk on how to keep believing in your dream and offer ways to keep yourself motivated on bad days.

14

Tricks to stay motivated

Now that you have all these nuts and bolts and pockets full of writing tools, how do you develop and keep faith in yourself, and keep the flame of your writing alive until you sell your first book? If you've already sold a book and are just in a bad stretch of your career, how do you hang on until you can sell the next one?

Writing novels and sustaining a writing career are not always easy undertakings; it seems that there is always someone saying how bad the business is just now. It's hard to get a book published, and just as hard to stay in the game. In this chapter, we will talk about ways to sustain your passion and keep yourself going, even when the going gets tough.

Staying the course

Writing is not an easy career. I've been engaged professionally as a novelist for 25 years and I've had great years and terrible years, and plodding years where it seems that the only thing I've done is write. There have been years when the sun was shining on me and years when it poured down rain. But there are no easy years.

Advances are dropping, they say, and old writers are being let go in favour of young blood. You have to know someone or do something drastic to get attention. Here's the terrible truth: it's always been that way; it's always going to be that way.

It can seem, when you are starting out, that a writer with a long career must have been charmed in some way, but trust me: there's little in the way of despair you can be feeling that I have not, at some time, known. When tell you to have faith, I can believe in what I'm saying because I have to use these techniques myself, over and over again.

 ## Anne Sullivan Macy

'Keep on beginning and failing. Each time you fail, start all over again, and you will grow stronger until you have accomplished a purpose... not the one you began with, perhaps, but one you'll be glad to remember.'

The opposite of faith in yourself is always fear. Fear is the great enemy of the creative person, and there are thousands of ways it attacks us. If you are discouraged, you are *dis*-couraged: faltering in courage; losing courage; letting fear get in your way.

Discouragement is faltering faith, the fear that you are not good enough to publish a novel or that it was fluke that you were published in the first place. You fear that the market is just not right for your kind of books right now and that it was a crazy idea to become a writer in the first place.

Discouragement is just a mask for your fear that you can't get what you want. I'm here to tell you that you can have whatever you want if you want it badly enough. The universe rewards determination and courage. In this chapter I'm going to talk about specific ways to renew your courage and get yourself going when your faith flags, but first, I think under these circumstances, it's important that you know a little about my story.

The road to publication

It's easy to think, when you've not yet seen your work in print, that every writer who is publishing was somehow born to be published. But of course no one is; getting published is hard for all of us. We have all had to fight to see our work in print, and to stay in print. As a once aspiring writer, I studied journalism at college because my father, who knew I wanted to write novels, feared for my security and urged me to study that subject. I was fairly good at it. I liked the work, talking to people, getting their stories, but it was always just a stopgap. I wanted to write fiction.

I worked in a bar through college and, one afternoon, I overheard a reporter I adored tell her friend that one day she was going to quit her job and write the great American novel. My heart stopped. It was a moment of absolute reckoning: if I did not write books now, I would never do it. I went home and asked my husband if he'd give me five years to sell a book. He gulped and said, 'OK.'

And, let me say, I wasn't going to go write for myself. I burned to *publish*. I had no desire whatsoever to write in my garret all alone. I burned – still do – to communicate ideas, thoughts, dreams and hopes to others. Communication is not completed until there is someone on the listening end. I was determined to figure out where I should be writing, and just kept trying venues: literary short stories, articles, novels, science fiction, then finally romance, which fitted my voice and passions like Cinderella's glass slipper.

Sometimes I despaired. Sometimes I cried. Sometimes it was hard for me to believe in myself enough to keep the naysayers from undermining me completely. The things that kept me going were a lot of the same kinds of things I hear other writers saying: I had something to prove. I wanted to prove to my father that writing novels was a good thing and could support me. I wanted to prove to my mother that I was a writer for real. I wanted to publish so that everyone would stop looking at me as if I were some pathetic misfit, and see that I was about something.

Key idea

Some of you, on your road to publication, will be asked to make sacrifices, without ever knowing what the outcome will be.

In 1988 I'd been seriously trying to publish for three years. There was a depression on in Pueblo, where I lived at the time. The steel mill industry had collapsed and the city was in dire straits. My husband was selling pizzas to keep a roof over our heads. I was taking care of my children and working in a bowling alley – and all the time, I had that journalism degree that would have made us a comfortable living with probably a few luxuries, too. But I knew, absolutely, that if I worked for the paper in the daytime, I'd never write my novels. I also knew that the one thing I couldn't bear in life was not giving it everything I had.

In 1988 I was close to despair. We didn't have a telephone and I was driving an ancient pick-up truck. I knew we couldn't hang on much longer. It was also the year of 'half-yeses', maybes and 'Let-me-see-it-agains'. Many of you may be enduring a year just like it: you know you're close; you can smell it, sense it and taste it. It's right there, just out of reach, like a pie on a windowsill above your head. This is the time when editors stop sending form letters and scrawled notes at the bottom of your query and start giving you some constructive criticism and encouragement. They say, 'I liked a lot of it, but not enough to buy it.' They say, 'Rewrite and I'll take another look.'

Then the promising note from an editor is followed by another rejection. Agony. It's a friend making her first sale and you've been writing longer. Agony. It's you writing longer than anyone else you know and you know that people are sometimes whispering behind your back, 'Why does she keep going?' The answer is: because you have to. It matters. And if you believe this for long enough, you will break through.

In 1988 my husband said to me one night: 'I don't think we can keep on like this much longer.' My father said, 'I know you believe, honey, but maybe some security wouldn't be such a bad thing.' Marge, the cook at the awful bowling alley where I slung beers for steelworkers who never tipped, said, 'People like us don't have dreams like that. You have a nice family.' (As I write this down, my eye starts to twitch.)

Keeping the flame alive

Where did I get the grit to believe in my work so much that I ignored absolutely every marker that said I was mad, ignored all the well-meaning people in my life, people who loved me and just wanted me to be happy, and stuck to this pie-in-the-sky dream of publishing books? If I go back to my journals from that period, I can see there were some specific things I was doing to keep the faith. They worked for me, so they should work for you, too.

1 STUDY YOUR GENRE

Study romance novels compulsively. I had a notebook and kept copious notes on my reading. I wasn't long out of college, so the obvious answer was to study things intensively, but I think people often skip this step.

When you feel discouraged, go back to the romance novels you think are brilliant and read them and take them apart to see what makes them work. You have the tools you need in this book. When I was studying the romantic novels I loved, it gave me something physical to do to understand how to make my work better.

Study is empowering. Study the craft, but do it in ways specific to you. Do your homework. If you feel frustrated, choose one thing to work on until you master it. When you have learned and mastered that one thing – say, dialogue – move on to the next thing.

2 SEEK OUT BIOGRAPHIES OF WRITERS AND ARTISTS

Seek out the work of the writers you admire and see whether you can find stories about their lives before they published. Remember, as you read them, that *they* didn't know they would be published either. One book that kept me going was about the short stories of Ursula K. Le Guin, about the history of each tale and who rejected it, and about her life before she eventually published at the ripe old age of 32. I thought that, if she'd been rejected that much, I could stand to be rejected, too.

Watch movies about writers and artists and their lives. *Shakespeare in Love* is a beauty – uplifting and moving.

The stories of other writers – how their lives and their work fit together – are inspiring. I love to read about women writers in earlier times and the struggles they faced. It makes me feel excited and a part of something bigger than myself.

3 KEEP YOUR SPIRITS UP WITH INSPIRING READS

Here are three books I have found motivating and return to again and again:

- *The Power of Positive Thinking* by Norman Vincent Peale
  One of the classics of the self-help genre, this book directly addresses the Judeo-Christian attachment to guilt and suffering. One of the reasons I still recommend it, even in a world that's now rather anti-Christian, is that, whatever your current

religious practices, by virtue of growing up in the Western world you have been affected by this to some degree or other. You may think in some way that it's more natural to suffer than to thrive. Peale doesn't think so. He says, 'Look at what God really says about success and achievement.'

- *The Artist's Way* by Julia Cameron
  Full of hundreds of inspiring phrases, this is the single most healing book ever written for creatives. I never get tired of it. It centres and grounds me and gives me courage when I am suffering discouragement. I have Cameronisms tacked up all over my office, including:
  o 'Keep the drama on the page', which works very well for discouragement, too
  o 'If I don't create I get crabby', which reminds me that the artist in me is a child (or even a baby) and needs spoiling, so that the outer me can cope with real life.

- *Walking on Water: Reflections on Faith and Art* by Madeleine L'Engle
  This is a passionate meditation on the nature of 'serving the work' you are given. It's unabashedly Christian and richly textured with her devotion to Christ, but in a loving way. She gave me one of my favourite ideas, which is that we are all asked to do more than we can do, and the trick is to serve the work as best we can. L'Engle makes writing a holy thing, an obligation; she says, 'If the work comes to you and says, "enflesh me", then you have an obligation to do your best. If you do not, the work might not ever get done.'

  Maybe it feels arrogant to think of your work like that. After all, how much holiness is there in a commercial fiction novel? But I choose to think of it in the opposite way. If the work is arriving to be 'enfleshed', then my job is to open the door, let it in, make it as comfortable as possible and do my best to help it continue the journey into the world. I'm a servant, not a god. It gives me courage to imagine serving the work like that.

 Write a fan letter

Who is your ideal reader? What does she look like? Where does she live? What does she get out of your books? Write a fan letter from her to you and be as lavish as you like.

4 GIVE YOURSELF ENCOURAGEMENT

One of the things I did when I was starting out and manuscripts came boomeranging back with depressing regularity was to type out any kind word I received from anyone and post it on my writing wall. If a rejection said I had a strong voice, I wrote, '*Redbook Magazine* says "You have a strong voice"' and put it up. Take every titbit you can find and hang it where you can see it.

Stick positive messages where you can see them

Write down every positive thing you've been told about your writing and put it on your wall where you can see it often when you are writing.

Affirmations, both written and – if you dare – spoken, are also a great way of focusing on the positive and offer another useful method of keeping yourself encouraged. If you are writing ten times a day, 'I'm a great writer', or 'I have all that I need to accomplish my dreams', you automatically bring more energy to whatever tasks you have in hand.

Record your affirmations

Record yourself speaking your affirmations aloud and listen to them as you meditate or cook dinner or take a walk. Your brain believes your voice more than it believes the voice of anyone else.

Try guided meditations. They clear out a lot of negativity and heal some of the wounds we carry. When you have a brutal rejection or a bad letter from a contest judge who just doesn't get your work, a guided meditation can get you back on track and believing in yourself.

5 SPEND TIME WITH PEOPLE WHO BRING OUT YOUR BEST

This seems obvious, but we all fall into patterns of surrounding ourselves with people who don't do us any good. The test is simple, however: if you feel good about your work and yourself after you spend time with someone, spend more time with them. If you feel bad about yourself after spending time with someone, spend less time with that person.

Hitting a career slump

What happens if you do get a book out there, get published, maybe even publish a lot of books, and then you find you hit a wall? You are feeling that you had your chance and you blew it, or the world blew it, or that publishing is no good and there's no point. How do you pick yourself up and keep going?

First of all, know that it is not unusual. Writers talk a lot about the successes in their careers, not so much about the failures, but most of your peers will have faced something bad: being orphaned by an editor or having a book published at the exact moment of a big disaster, such as Hurricane Katrina or a massive ice storm that cancels all travel (and thus all shipping), during a release week. A million things can happen.

All of the above tricks for keeping the faith will help, but what I do at such turning points is go back underground to write a whole book. The only thing I know better than agents, editors and publishing is that I am the writer. I know what I'm doing. They might know all kinds of things about marketing, distribution and current trends, but what *I* know is how to write a novel. It might not be the novel of the moment. It might not be the novel a particular editor wants to read this week or this month or this year. It might not be the kind of book that will put me on the *New York Times* bestseller list and make me into a razzle-dazzle star.

But I know how to write a novel. I know how to write my kind of novel. I will make you cry until you are sobbing in the middle of a pool of tears at your table. I go over the top. I know how to write a redemption story that will make you believe in yourself and your world again.

And here's what else I know: you've published novels, and you know how to write your kind of book, too. Maybe your special gift is magical worlds. Maybe it's military thrillers. Maybe it's erotica so hot it singes fingers.

Whatever it is, you know what you do best. You know how to write novels. The editors don't know. The agents don't know. The readers don't know. You know. Take your work back. Shut out those voices of criticism that are telling you that you're a loser, a has-been, a nothing, and tell them that they don't know what they're talking about.

Conversely, don't be afraid to start over, to start afresh, to do something completely new and different.

Just write

Whatever else you do: write. Write every day if you can. Keep writing. Keep writing. Keep writing. Life is long. Careers are long. Things shift and shift again. If you keep writing, you will get to a place where you find your right fit.

If you stop writing, though, I can guarantee that you won't. Your dream will die. Your books will go unwritten.

Ray Bradbury

'You fail only if you stop writing.'

Writing and publishing books is a great life, and it's worth pursuing. For all that publishing makes me crazy some days and the way the money flows is not for the faint of heart, it's a great life. Writing is excellent, and so is seeing the work in the world, doing whatever it is going to do.

Have courage. Stay the course.

References

Aaron, Rachel, *2K to 10K: Writing Faster, Writing Better, and Writing More of What You Love* (Rachel Aaron, 2013)

Aftel, Mandy, *Essence and Alchemy* (Gibbs M. Smith, 2004)

Cameron, Julia, *The Artist's Way* (Pan, 1995)

The Chicago Manual of Style (Chicago Press, 2010)

Gordon, Karen Elizabeth, *The Transitive Vampire* (Pantheon, 1993)

Kinsale, Laura, *The Shadow and the Star* (HarperCollins, 1991)

L'Engle, Madeleine, *Walking on Water: Reflections on Faith and Art* (Waterbrook Press, 2001)

McKee, Robert, *Story* (HarperCollins e-books, 2010)

Moore, Susanna, *One Last Look* (Vintage, 2004)

O'Neal, Barbara, *The Lost Recipe for Happiness* (Bantam Books, 2008)

The Oxford Manual of Style (Oxford University Press, 2002)

Peale, Norman Vincent, *The Power of Positive Thinking* (Vermilion, 1990)

Samuel, Barbara, *Lucien's Fall* (HarperCollins, 1995; e-book, 2011)

Samuel, Barbara, *No Place Like Home* (Ballantine Books, 2002)

Schmidt, Victoria Lynn, *45 Master Characters* (Writer's Digest Books, 2001)

Vogler, Christopher, *The Writer's Journey* (Pan Books, 1999)

Appendix 1: A list of 100 best romantic novels

From Buzzle.com
 1 *A Countess below Stairs* by Eva Ibbotson
 2 *A Knight in Shining Armor* by Jude Deveraux
 3 *A Room with a View* by E.M. Forster
 4 *A Summer to Remember* by Mary Balogh
 5 *According to Jane* by Marilyn Brant
 6 *Angelique and the King* by Sergeanne Golon, Anne Golon
 7 *Angelique* by Sergeanne Golon
 8 *Angelique in Barbary* by Sergeanne Golon, Anne Golon
 9 *Bet Me* by Jennifer Crusie
10 *Catching Fire* by Suzanne Collins
11 *Christy* by Catherine Marshall
12 *Comanche Moon* by Catherine Anderson
13 *Cotillion* by Georgette Heyer
14 *Danger in the Shadows* by Dee Henderson
15 *Daughter of the Forest* by Juliet Marillier
16 *Dawn's Early Light* by Elswyth Thane
17 *Devil in Winter* by Lisa Kleypas
18 *Dragonfly in Amber* by Diana Gabaldon
19 *Dream Man* by Linda Howard
20 *Dreaming of You* by Lisa Kleypas
21 *Family Blessings* by LaVyrle Spencer
22 *Flowers from the Storm* by Laura Kinsale
23 *Forever Amber* by Kathleen Winsor
24 *Frederica* by Georgette Heyer
25 *From This Day* by Nora Roberts
26 *Garden Spells* by Sarah Addison Allen
27 *Gone with the Wind* by Margaret Mitchell
28 *Heaven, Texas* by Susan Elizabeth Phillips
29 *Honor's Splendour* by Julie Garwood
30 *I Capture the Castle* by Dodie Smith
31 *It Had to Be You* by Susan Elizabeth Phillips

71 *The Hunger Games* by Suzanne Collins
72 *The Madness of Lord Ian Mackenzie* by Jennifer Ashley
73 *The Manny* by Holly Peterson
74 *The Morning Gift* by Eva Ibbotson
75 *The Nonesuch* by Georgette Heyer
76 *The Notebook* by Nicholas Sparks
77 *The Phantom of the Opera* by Gaston Leroux
78 *The Princess* by Lori Wick
79 *The Prize* by Julie Garwood
80 *The Quiet Gentleman* by Georgette Heyer
81 *The Rake* by Mary Jo Putney
82 *The Raven Prince* by Elizabeth Hoyt
83 *The Reluctant Widow* by Georgette Heyer
84 *The Secret* by Julie Garwood
85 *The Secret Pearl* by Mary Balogh
86 *The Shell Seekers* by Rosamunde Pilcher
87 *The Song of the Lioness Quartet* by Tamora Pierce
88 *The Struggle* by L.J. Smith
89 *The Summer Before the Dark* by Doris Lessing
90 *The Thorn Birds* by Colleen McCullough
91 *The Unknown Ajax* by Georgette Heyer
92 *The Wolf and the Dove* by Kathleen E. Woodiwiss
93 *These Old Shades* by Georgette Heyer
94 *Truly Madly Yours* by Rachel Gibson
95 *Wake* by Lisa McMann
96 *When the Splendor Falls* by Laurie McBain
97 *Where Dreams Begin* by Lisa Kleypas
98 *Whitney, My Love* by Judith McNaught
99 *Wuthering Heights* by Emily Brontë
100 *Years* by LaVyrle Spencer

Read more at Buzzle: www.buzzle.com/articles/best-romance-novels-of-all-time.html

Appendix 2: Romance Writers of America: RWA hall of fame winners

For the most current list, go to www.rwa.org/p/cm/ld/fid=555

Kresley Cole
Paranormal Romance
Qualifying novels:
2007 – *A Hunger Like No Other*
2010 – *Kiss of a Demon King*
2013 – *Shadow's Claim*

Karen Templeton
Contemporary Series Romance
Qualifying novels:
2009 – *A Mother's Wish*
2011 – *Welcome Home, Cowboy*
2013 – *A Gift for All Seasons*

Barbara O'Neal
Novel with Strong Romantic Elements
Qualifying novels:
2006 – *Lady Luck's Map of Vegas*
2010 – *The Lost Recipe for Happiness*
2012 – *How to Bake a Perfect Life*

Julia Quinn
Regency Historical Romance
Qualifying novels:
2007 – *On the Way to the Wedding*
2008 – *The Secret Diaries of Miss Miranda Cheever*
2010 – *What Happens in London*

Kathleen Creighton
Contemporary Series Romance
Qualifying novels:
1988 – *In the Defense of Love*
2004 – *The Top Gun's Return*
2009 – *Danger Signals*

Jodi Thomas
Short Historical Romance
Qualifying novels:
1992 – *The Tender Texan*
1995 – *To Tame a Texan's Heart*
2006 – *The Texan's Reward*

Susan Elizabeth Phillips
Contemporary Single Title
Qualifying novels:
1998 – *Nobody's Baby But Mine*
1999 – *Dream a Little Dream*
2001 – *First Lady*

Nora Roberts
Long Contemporary Romance
Qualifying novels:
1983 – *The Heart's Victory*
1984 – *This Magic Moment*
1985 – *A Matter of Choice*
1987 – *One Summer*

LaVyrle Spencer
Single Title Historical Romance
Qualifying novels:
1983 – *The Endearment*
1984 – *Hummingbird*
1985 – *Twice Loved*
1988 – *The Gamble*

Nora Roberts
Romantic Suspense
Qualifying novels:
1989 – *Brazen Virtue*
1992 – *Night Shift*
1993 – *Divine Evil*
1994 – *Nightshade*
1995 – *Hidden Riches*

Jo Beverley
Regency Romance
Qualifying novels:
1992 – *Emily and the Dark Angel*
1993 – *An Unwilling Bride*
1994 – *Deirdre and Don Juan*

Kathleen Korbel (Eileen Dreyer)
Long Contemporary Romance
Qualifying novels:
1990 – *The Ice Cream Man*
1992 – *A Rose for Maggie*
1995 – *A Soldier's Heart*

Nora Roberts
Contemporary Single Title Romance
Qualifying novels:
1991 – *Public Secrets*
1994 – *Private Scandals*
1996 – *Born in Ice*

Cheryl Zach
Young Adult Romance
Qualifying novels:
1985 – *The Frog Princess*
1986 – *Waiting for Amanda*
1996 – *Runaway*

Francine Rivers

Inspirational Romance

Qualifying novels:

1995 – *An Echo in the Darkness*

1996 – *As Sure as the Dawn*

1997 – *The Scarlet Thread*

Jennifer Greene (Alison Hart)

Short Contemporary Series Romance

Qualifying novels:

1990 – *Night of the Hunter*

1996 – *Single Dad*

1998 – *Nobody's Princess*

Justine Dare (Justine Davis/Janice Davis Smith)

Paranormal Romance

Qualifying novels:

1991 – *Angel for Hire (Justine Davis)*

1995 – *Lord of the Storm*

1998 – *Fire Hawk*

Appendix 3: My own favourite romantic novels

Some of these might not have perfectly happy endings or fit RWA's definitions of a romance, but this is my list, and it includes a wide variety of novels, in no particular order, from quite traditional to very untraditional. To be a spectacular romantic story, according to my criteria, the book must be intelligent and well written, with characters I care deeply about and a romance that feels true, whether it ends happily ever after or not. Often my favourite of a writer's work is not the book for which they are best known or most beloved.

- *Green Darkness* by Anya Seton
- *On the Night of the Seventh Moon* by Victoria Holt
- *The Time Traveler's Wife* by Audrey Niffeneger
- *The Shadow and The Star* by Laura Kinsale
- *Flowers From The Storm* by Laura Kinsale
- *The Thorn Birds* by Colleen McCollough
- *Night of the Phantom* by Anne Stuart
- *Bet Me* by Jennifer Crusie
- *Devil's Bride* by Stephanie Laurens
- *Wish You Were Here* by Christie Ridgway
- *Uncommon Vows* by Mary Jo Putney
- *The Bride and the Beast* by Teresa Medieros
- *Daniel's Gift* by Barbara Freethy
- *The Shattered Rose* by Jo Beverly
- *Not Quite a Husband* by Sherry Thomas
- *The Portrait* by Megan Chance
- *White Horses* by Alice Hoffman
- *The Fault in Our Stars* by John Green
- *Garden Spells* by Sarah Addison Allen
- *Like Water for Chocolate* by Laura Esquivel
- *If I Stay* by Gayle Forman
- *Slammed* by Colleen Hoover
- *Eleanor and Park* by Rainbow Rowell
- *Me Before You* by Jo Jo Moyes

Appendix 4: Find out more

Here are some links to more information online:

- Romance Writers of America: http://www.rwa.org
- Romance Writers of Australia: http://www.romanceaustralia.com
- Romance Writers of New Zealand: http://www.romancewriters.co.nz
- Romantic Writers of United Kingdom: http://www.rna-uk.org
- Women's Fiction Writers: https://womensfictionwriters.org
- RT Book Reviews http://www.rtbookreviews.com
- Smart Bitches, Trashy Novels: http://www.smartbitchestrashybooks.com
- Dear Author: http://dearauthor.com
- Harlequin Author Pages (source for guidelines for their various books): http://www.harlequin.com/articlepage.html?articleId=538&chapter=0
- Show Me The Money (information on income): http://brendahiatt.com/show-me-the-money/

Index